The Famous Five and You
Search for Smugglers

4

Join the Famous Five on their mysterious
visit to Smuggler's Top where strange
happenings result in an unlikely
disappearance. Discover a maze of secret
passages and trace the path you think the
Five should take to rescue the fugitives
and reveal the sinister smugglers. Will you
go straight to them, or will you take a
false trail along the way?

This exciting game story is based on Enid
Blyton's *Five Go to Smuggler's Top*.

Join the action in
The Famous Five and You!

Enid Blyton, who died in 1968 at the age of 71 became, during her lifetime, Britain's best-loved and most popular author, and is still considered to have wielded a greater influence than any other author over children's writing in the post-war years. She loved young people, and wrote for 'all children, any children, everywhere' – over 600 books, many songs, poems and plays.

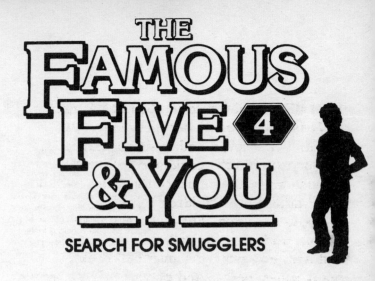

THE FAMOUS FIVE & YOU 4

SEARCH FOR SMUGGLERS

An Enid Blyton story
devised and adapted
by Mary Danby

Based on Enid Blyton's
Five Go to Smuggler's Top

Illustrated by Kate Rogers

KNIGHT BOOKS
Hodder and Stoughton

Text copyright © 1988 Mary
Danby/Darrell Waters Limited
Illustrations copyright © 1988
Hodder and Stoughton Limited

*First published in Great Britain in
1988 by Knight Books*

Enid Blyton is a Trade Mark of
Darrell Waters Limited

British Library C.I.P.

Danby, Mary, *1941–*
Search for smugglers.
1. Adventure games – For children
I. Title
II. Rogers, Kate
III. Blyton Enid,
Five go to smuggler's top
IV. Series
793'.9

ISBN 0-340-42617-9

Printed and bound in Great Britain for
Hodder and Stoughton Paperbacks, a
division of Hodder and Stoughton
Limited, Mill Road, Dunton Green,
Sevenoaks, Kent TN13 2YA.
(Editorial Office: 47 Bedford Square,
London WC1B 3DP) by Cox and
Wyman Limited, Reading, Berks.
Photoset by Rowland
Phototypesetting Limited, Bury St
Edmunds, Suffolk.

THE FAMOUS FIVE – AND YOU

Unlike an ordinary book, which you can read straight through from beginning to end, this is a gamebook, in which *you* choose how the story should go.

Begin at paragraph number 1. At the end of each paragraph you are told which paragraph to read next. Sometimes you will find you have a choice. (For instance, at the end of paragraph 7 you have to decide whether or not the Famous Five should speak to the man on the train.)

Every time you have a choice to make, there will be one way that is the quickest and best – and you have to guess (or work out, if you can) which it is. If you choose the wrong paragraph, you can still carry on reading, but when you find yourself back at the main story you will find you have picked up a few 'red herrings'.

A red herring is the name given to something that carries you away from the main subject (as when someone is telling you a story and puts in all sorts of details that don't really matter). Your aim is to try and stay on the main track, without going off down the little side roads.

See if you can make the right choices and find

your way to the end of the story without picking up too many red herrings. A red herring is shown by this symbol: ⌒⊲. Use a pencil and paper to add up your score as you go along, then turn to the back of the book to see how well The Famous Five (and You) have done.

1

One fine day at the beginning of the Easter holidays, four children and a dog travelled by train to the seaside village of Kirrin. The four were Julian, Dick, Anne and their cousin Georgina, always known as George. The black and white dog, who belonged to George, was called Timmy.

'Soon be there!' exclaimed Julian with satisfaction as the train drew to a halt. 'This is the last stop before Kirrin!'

The cousins were going to spend the holidays with George and her parents, Uncle Quentin and Aunt Fanny, who lived at Kirrin Cottage, a lovely old house not far from the sea.

Go to **7**.

2

Soon they were all sitting around the table eating a big tea. Aunt Fanny always had a large meal waiting for them when they first arrived, for she knew they would be very hungry after their long journey.

'I hope the wind will die down tonight,' she said. 'It kept me awake last night. Julian, you're looking rather thin. Have you been working hard? I must try to build you up.'

They all laughed.

'Just what we thought you'd say, Mother!' said George. 'Goodness, what's that?'

There was a large bumping noise on the roof. They all sat still, startled.

'I expect a tile has blown off,' said Uncle Quentin.

'It sounded heavier than that,' said George. 'We'd better go and look.'

If you think it was a tile, go to **12**.
If you think it was something else, go to **17**.

3

'Come on, Dick, we're all waiting for that last two of hearts,' said George.

'All right, I'm being as quick as I can,' said Dick.

Julian and Anne each slapped a card on a pile at the same moment.

'I got there first!' said Anne.

'No, you didn't!' said Julian. 'I did!'

'No, you *didn't*!' said Anne.

The four of them got crosser and crosser as they played. They were all tired and irritable after their long journey. They were making a lot of noise, too, and suddenly the door flew open and Uncle Quentin came in.

'What do you all mean by making so much noise?'

he demanded. 'How can I concentrate on my reading with this racket going on? Now get off to bed, all of you!'

The children sorted out the cards and put them away, then said goodnight to Aunt Fanny.

Go to **11**.

4

If you've arrived from **10**, *score* ◁.

The four children and Timmy tumbled out of the train. George's mother was on the platform to meet them. They piled all the luggage into the pony-trap and set off for Kirrin Cottage. It was very blustery and cold, and the children pulled their coats tightly around them.

'The wind has been very strong the last day or two,' said Aunt Fanny. 'The fishermen have pulled their boats high on the beach for fear of a big storm.'

The children could see the boats pulled right up as they passed the beach where they had so often bathed.

'Look!' said Anne, who had sharp eyes. 'Look! One of the boats is drifting out to sea!'

'Quick, Mother, stop!' cried George. 'We'd better go and see if there's anything we can do.'

'I really think we'd better go on, dear,' said her mother. 'Your father will worry if we're late.'

If you think they should stop, go to **9**.
If you think they should go on, go to **15**.

'Do you know a boy called Pierre Lenoir?' asked Uncle Quentin suddenly, taking a letter from his pocket. 'I believe he goes to your school, boys.'

'Pierre Lenoir – oh, you mean old Sooty,' replied Julian. 'Yes – he's in Dick's form. Mad as a hatter.'

'Sooty! Now why do you call him that?' said Uncle Quentin. 'It seems a silly name for a boy.'

'If you saw him you wouldn't think so,' said Dick with a laugh. 'He's awfully dark! Hair as black as soot, eyes like bits of coal, eyebrows that look as if they've been drawn on with charcoal. And his name means "the black one", doesn't it? Noir – that's French for black.'

'Oh, well, that explains it,' said Uncle Quentin. 'Well, I've been corresponding with this boy's father. We are both interested in the same scientific matters, and I've asked him whether he wouldn't like to come and stay with me for a few days – and bring his boy, Pierre.'

The children thought that having Sooty Lenoir to stay might be fun!

Go to **16**.

'Supposing it falls on someone's head,' said Aunt Fanny. 'I really think that we should try to get it down, Quentin.'

'Very well,' said Uncle Quentin. 'Julian, would you please get the ladder from the outhouse.'

'Right,' said Julian, and shot off. He was back in a minute carrying a light metal ladder, which he propped up against the gutter.

'Dick, you and George hold the ladder steady, and I'll climb up,' said Julian.

His uncle and aunt watched anxiously as Julian climbed the ladder, and, leaning forwards, caught hold of the piece of chimney-pot. He had just about got it free from the guttering when suddenly Timmy dashed into the yard in hot pursuit of the kitchen cat. George's attention was distracted for a moment, and, at the same time, the wind suddenly blew a tremendously strong gust. The ladder wobbled sickeningly for a moment, then crashed to the ground!

Go to **14**.

7

A few people got into the carriage, and then the whistle blew and the train pulled out of the station.

Anne began to cough, and couldn't stop.

'What's the matter, Anne?' asked Julian. 'Are you getting a cold?'

'No,' said Anne between coughs. 'It's the smoke from that man's cigarette.'

Not far from them sat a man in a grey suit. His

hair was very fair, almost white, and his pink face had a scar that ran from his eye right down to the corner of his cross-looking mouth. He was puffing on a cigarette, and the open carriage window was sending the smoke in Anne's direction.

They all stared at him.

'But this is a non-smoker,' objected Dick in a low voice. 'It says so on the window.'

George peered at the man. 'Should we ask him to stop smoking?' she wondered. 'He doesn't look a very friendly type to me.'

If you think they should speak to the man, go to **13**.
If you think they shouldn't say anything, go to **18**.

8

'Oh, let's play Racing Demon, Aunt Fanny!' begged Anne. 'I do like it!'

'The reason you like it so much is because you know you can beat the rest of us,' said Julian with a grin.

He was quite right. Anne had quick eyes and nimble fingers, and it was difficult for any of the others to beat her.

George went to get the cards from the dining-room.

'I can only find four packs,' she said when she came back, 'and we need a pack each for this game.'

'That's all right, dear,' said her mother. 'I shall be quite happy to sit and watch. I'll do my knitting.'

They all shuffled their cards, then Julian held up his hand.

'Right,' he said. 'One, two, three, go!'

They all started turning cards over, pushing aces into the centre as quickly as they could, and trying to keep an eye on their own and everyone else's cards at the same time.

Go to **3**.

9

'We *must* stop, Mother!' said George. 'I think that's Alf's boat. We've got to do something to help.' Alf was a fisherman who had done many good turns for them. Now perhaps they could do one for him.

Aunt Fanny pulled the pony to a halt, and the four children jumped out and ran towards the beach.

'How are we going to get hold of it?' panted Dick as he ran.

'I'll swim out and grab hold of its rope,' said George.

'You can't swim in this weather, George,' said Julian. 'I know you're a strong swimmer, but the sea is much too rough!'

Just then an extra-large wave threw the boat up high, and they could all see that it had not been drifting after all. A long rope, attached to the stern, ran up the beach to an iron ring in the sea wall.

'Oh, thank goodness,' said George. 'All that's

happened is that the rope has come unwound. We can pull the boat in and wind the rope up again, and it'll be fine.'

They all pulled hard on the rope, and soon the boat was sliding up the beach, well out of the rough, angry sea. George secured the rope in a neat coil, and they climbed back into the trap.

Go to **15**.

10

The man with the cigarette glared at Julian.

'Certainly not!' he said. 'If I wish to smoke I shall do so. A boy of your age has no business telling a grown-up what to do. Now just go back to your seat.'

'I really do think you should put that cigarette out,' said Julian, 'but if you won't listen to me perhaps I'd better go and find the guard.'

The man gave Julian an angry stare, then got to his feet. 'I'll remember you,' he said nastily, before moving to another part of the train.

'Well,' said Julian as he sat down again, 'that's that!'

'Goodness,' said Anne. 'You are brave, Julian.'

Soon the train began to slow down, and the children pulled their cases from the rack. The station name – K-I-R-R-I-N – slid past the window.

Go to **4**.

11

If you've arrived from **3**, *score* ⌒.

It was nice to climb up the steep stairs to their familiar bedrooms that night. They were all yawning widely.

'If only this awful wind would stop!' said Anne, pulling the curtain aside and looking out into the night.

'I'm jolly cold,' said George, scrambling into bed. 'Hurry, Anne, or you'll catch a chill at that window.'

'Don't the waves make a noise?' said Anne, still at the window. 'And the gale in the old ash tree is making a whistling, howling sound and bending the tree right over.'

She got into bed and lay down.

'Good night,' said George sleepily. 'I hope that Sooty boy comes, don't you? He sounds rather fun.'

Go to **24**.

12

If you've arrived from **23**, *score* ⌒ ⌒ .
If you've arrived from **19**, *score* ⌒ ⌒ ⌒ ⌒.

'You all stay here,' said Uncle Quentin. 'I'll go and have a look.'

He was back in a minute or two.

'Just a tile,' he said, 'but we shall have to get it seen to when the storm is over, Fanny.'

The children rather hoped that their uncle would retire to his study after tea, as he usually did, but this time he didn't. He sat on at the table, asking them questions about their schools.

Go to **5**.

13

Anne looked a bit doubtful, though the smoke was still making her cough.

'Do you think we ought to?' she asked. 'After all, an adult might not take very much notice of one of us. Perhaps we should wait until the guard comes along.'

'Nonsense!' said Julian. 'Of course we can ask him to stop. This is a non-smoking carriage, after all.' He got up and walked over to where the man was sitting.

'Excuse me, sir,' he said, 'but would you mind putting your cigarette out? It's making my sister cough – and this *is* a non-smoking carriage.'

Go to **10**.

14

Anne gave a shriek and burst into tears. Julian was sprawled on the ground, the ladder on top of him, and the piece of chimney-pot in his hands.

'Julian!' cried Aunt Fanny. 'Julian, are you all right? Quick, Quentin, pull the ladder off him.'

Uncle Quentin and Dick pulled the ladder off Julian, who was lying motionless, his eyes closed. Aunt Fanny and Anne bent over him anxiously.

'Julian, say something, please!' begged Anne.

Much to their relief Julian opened his eyes and sat up slowly.

'Are you all right?' asked Aunt Fanny again. 'Can you move your arms and legs? Have you hurt your head?'

Go to **19**.

15

If you've arrived from **9**, *score* ⌒.

Aunt Fanny clicked to the pony and the trap moved forwards.

The children continued to watch the boat anxiously. Then George gave a shout: 'Look! There's one of the fishermen come to check on the boats. It'll be all right – he'll see to that.'

The wind howled over the sea. Great scudding clouds raced overhead. The waves pounded on the beach and made a terrific noise. Anne felt a bit scared, but the other three thought the rough weather was rather exciting.

'Here we are!' said Julian, as the trap stopped outside Kirrin Cottage.

Uncle Quentin came out to help with the luggage. He was a tall man, with a rather stern face, who looked like a scientist – which is what he was. He needed peace and quiet for his work, and often flew into a temper when he didn't get it, or when things didn't go the way he wanted. The children never felt as comfortable with him as they did with their gentle Aunt Fanny.

Go to **2**.

16

Much to the children's relief Uncle Quentin soon retired to read by himself. Aunt Fanny looked at the clock.

'Time for Anne to go to bed,' she said. 'And you too, George.'

'Just one good game of Racing Demon, all of us playing it together, Mother!' said George. 'Come on – you play it too. One good game, and then we'll go to bed. Even Julian's yawning.'

'I think Racing Demon might be too rowdy,' objected Aunt Fanny. 'You always make a lot of noise when you play it, and we don't want to disturb your father. I think we'd better play Rummy.'

'Oh, Mother, please let's play Racing Demon!' begged George. 'You know how much we all enjoy it.'

Aunt Fanny sighed. 'Now, George,' she said, 'think how your father hates noise . . .'

If you think they should play Rummy, go to **20**.
If you think they should play Racing Demon, go to **8**.

They all went outside and walked around the house, looking up at the roof to see if a tile had come off.

Suddenly Dick gave a shout. 'Come and look at this, everyone!'

He was standing staring up at the angle of the roof where the kitchen met the scullery. A large piece from one of the chimney-pots was wedged over the guttering. Glancing higher up, they could see that one of the chimney-pots had blown over and been smashed.

'Oh, goodness!' exclaimed Aunt Fanny. 'Now what are we going to do about that?'

'Perhaps we'd better get a ladder and climb up and remove it,' suggested Julian.

'That could be dangerous in this wind,' said his uncle. 'It might be best to leave it until the storm is over.'

If you think they should get a ladder, go to **6**.
If you think they should leave it, go to **23**.

18

They looked at each other, wondering what to do. Anne wasn't coughing so badly now.

'I don't think it's worth saying anything,' said Dick. 'After all, we're getting out at the next station.'

'Yes, but it isn't right for someone to smoke in a non-smoking carriage,' complained Julian.

Just then, however, the man who was smoking suddenly looked up at the window, saw the No Smoking sign and hurriedly put his cigarette out.

'Well,' said Julian, 'that's all right. Come on, pick up your things – we're nearly there!'

Soon the train began to slow down. The station name – K-I-R-R-I-N – slid past the window.

Go to **4**.

19

Julian shook his head gently, then felt it all over.

'I've got rather a bump on the back of my head,'

he said, 'but I don't think anything else has been damaged!'

'Stand up and see if you can walk all right,' said Aunt Fanny. 'In fact, I think we'd better get you into the house, and perhaps I'd better call Dr Poole.'

'Oh, no,' said Julian, walking rather shakily into the kitchen, 'I'm quite certain I don't need a doctor, Aunt Fanny. I'm fine, really I am.'

'Well, I think you'd better sit down quietly on the sofa for a while and rest,' said his aunt. 'If your head starts to ache, or you feel sick or drowsy, make sure you tell me.'

Julian lay down on the sofa with relief. He hadn't hurt himself, but he did feel rather shaken! The others all sat round talking quietly. The noise of the wind grew louder and louder, and there was another loud crash.

'I wonder if that's a tile, or another piece of the chimney-pot?' said George.

Go to **12**.

20

George looked rebellious for a moment, then smiled. 'All right, Mother, I don't mind playing Rummy,' she said. 'Now – where are the cards? Are they still in the drawer in the dining-room?'

'I think so,' said Aunt Fanny, and George went to get them.

They had one game, then decided there was just time for one more before bed.

'Right,' said Aunt Fanny. 'Off to bed with you all. The same bedrooms as usual, of course. Good night!'

Go to **11**.

21

If you've arrived from **35***, score* ⌒ *.*

But Aunt Fanny was wrong. The gale didn't blow itself out that night. Instead it raged around the house even more fiercely, shrieking and howling like a living thing. Nobody could sleep. Timmy kept up a continuous low growling – he didn't like the shakes and rattles and howls.

Towards dawn the wind seemed in a fury. Anne thought it sounded as if it was in a horrible temper, out to do all the harm it could. She lay and trembled, half-frightened.

Suddenly there was a strange noise. It was a loud and woeful groaning and creaking. The two girls sat up, terrified. What could it be?

The boys heard it too. Julian leapt out of bed and ran to the window. Outside stood the old ash tree, tall and black in the fitful moonlight. It was gradually bending over!

If you think the ash tree falls on the house, go to **27***.*
If you think it doesn't, go to **33***.*

If you've arrived from **30**, *score* 🐟 🐟.

'Oh, all right,' said Aunt Fanny. 'You can all sleep in the same room. But not too much talking, mind!'

The four children and Timmy settled down in the sitting-room. They found it very difficult to get to sleep after all the excitement, but eventually they dropped off.

Next morning the wind was still strong, but the fury of the storm had gone. In the light of day it was surprising to see what damage the big tree had done. It had cracked the roof of the house like an eggshell, and the upstairs rooms were in a terrible state.

'The first thing to do is to decide what to do with you children,' said Uncle Quentin. 'After breakfast we'll talk things over.'

Just at that moment they heard someone coming through the front gate.

'That'll be the postman, I expect,' said Julian. 'Shall I go?'

He got up from the table and in a moment came back with a letter in his hand. 'It's for you, Uncle Quentin,' he said.

'Who is it from?' asked Aunt Fanny.

'It looks rather like my father's writing,' said Julian.

Uncle Quentin frowned. 'I'm expecting a letter from Mr Lenoir.'

If you think the letter is from Julian's father, go to **28**.
If you think it's from Mr Lenoir, go to **40**.

23

They watched anxiously to see if any more bits were going to fall off the damaged chimney-pot. Suddenly there was another terribly strong gust of wind, and the piece of chimney-pot fell from the gutter into the yard with a loud crash!

'Lucky none of us were standing underneath!' exclaimed Dick.

'Well, there's nothing we can do about that chimney-pot now,' said Aunt Fanny. 'Come back into the house and get warm.'

They were all sitting by the fire, talking about their plans for the holidays, when there was another loud crash.

'I wonder if that was another piece of the chimney-pot, or a tile?' said Aunt Fanny.

Go to **12**.

24

Suddenly a loud bang made both girls jump.

'That's the bedroom door,' said George with a groan. 'One of the boys must have left it open. It's the sort of noise that drives Father mad! There it goes again!'

'Well, let Julian or Dick shut it,' said Anne, who

was beginning to feel nice and warm. 'After all, they left it open.'

'They're probably lying in bed waiting for one of us to get up and close it,' replied George. 'Oh, bother! Shall I get up? I don't want to, I'm feeling so cosy, but Father will get cross if that noise goes on.'

If you think George should get up, go to **29**.
If you think she should stay in bed, go to **39**.

25

The four children went into Uncle Quentin's study.

'I've spoken to Mr Lenoir,' he said, 'and he'll be happy to have you at Smuggler's Top.'

'*Smuggler's Top!*' exclaimed Dick. 'What's that?'

'The name of his house,' said Uncle Quentin. 'It's built on top of a strange hill surrounded by marshes over which the sea once flowed. Apparently a lot of smuggling used to go on there in the old days. It's a very peculiar place, I believe. Well – would you like to go? I'm afraid the only alternative would be for you to go back to school. I assume there'd be someone there who could keep an eye on you.'

Of course, they were all delighted at the idea of going to Smuggler's Top. It sounded simply thrilling.

'Can I take Timmy?' asked George eagerly.

'No,' said her father. 'I'm afraid Mr Lenoir doesn't like dogs.'

'I won't go without Timmy,' said George crossly.

'I'd rather go back to school. At least I can have him with me there.'

'No sulks, please, George,' said Uncle Quentin. 'Now, off you all go and start to pack. I've hired a car to take you to Smuggler's Top this morning.'

The children left the study and went upstairs, where Aunt Fanny helped them to pack. It was impossible to get some of the things from the girls' room, because the tree was in the way.

'George! You simply must come with us,' said Anne, as they opened their cases on the landing. 'I can't bear to think of you going back to school all alone.'

'I shouldn't be alone,' said George. 'I should have Timmy.'

She sat on the top step of the staircase, thinking hard, a deep scowl on her face.

Go to **36**.

26

The car sped on, mostly along the coast, though it sometimes went inland for a few miles. At half-past twelve the driver stopped at an old inn, and they all trooped inside. They had a delicious meal and Timmy had a large plate of scraps. After lunch they went into the kitchen to see the innkeeper and his wife.

'I hear you're going to Castaway,' said the innkeeper. 'You be careful there!'

'Castaway!' said Julian. 'Is that what the hill is called where Smuggler's Top is? Why do you say we should be careful?'

'Because there's only one good road across the marsh, and if you wander off it, the marsh will suck you down!' replied the innkeeper.

Anne gave a shiver. She didn't like that idea very much!

'Time to get on,' said their driver, looking at the clock. 'Your uncle said I was to get you there by teatime.'

Go to **38**.

27

If you've arrived from **33**, *score* ◁.

'It's the big tree! It's falling!' yelled Julian, almost startling Dick out of his wits. 'It's falling, I tell you. It'll crash on the house! Quick, warn the girls!'

Shouting at the top of his voice, Julian raced out of his door on to the landing. 'Uncle! Aunt! George and Anne! Come downstairs quickly! A tree is falling!'

George jumped out of bed, snatched up her dressing-gown and raced to the door, yelling to Anne, who was scrambling hurriedly out of bed. Timmy ran in front of them. On the landing they met Julian and Dick, Uncle Quentin and Aunt Fanny. They all fled downstairs as, with an appalling wail, the great tree hauled up its roots and fell heavily on to the roof of Kirrin Cottage. There was a

terrible crash, then the sound of tiles falling to the ground. Then there were other noises, thuds and little smashing sounds. The children couldn't imagine what was happening. Eventually the noises stopped.

Uncle Quentin took a torch and went carefully up the stairs to the landing to see what damage had been done. He came back looking very pale.

Go to **37**.

28

Uncle Quentin tore the letter open and glanced quickly at the contents.

'It's from your father,' he said to Julian. 'It's just a quick note to say that they will be away for about a fortnight. Obviously we can't send you home, so I don't quite know what we're going to do with you all. You can't stay here, that's for certain.'

At that moment the doorbell rang. Uncle Quentin, who had finished his breakfast, got up.

'I'll see who that is,' he said. 'You children finish eating.'

The children sat in silence. Nobody was feeling very hungry. They couldn't stay at Kirrin Cottage, they couldn't go home because their parents were away. It almost looked as if they would have to go back to school.

Just then Uncle Quentin reappeared with a letter in his hand. 'The postman had to come back. He dropped this letter on the drive.'

'Who is it from?' asked Aunt Fanny.

Go to **40**.

29

The door gave another loud bang. George jumped out of bed and ran down the passage to close it.

'Brr!' she said, scrambling back into bed as fast as she could. 'It's jolly cold out there!'

The gale still roared. Uncle Quentin and Aunt Fanny came up to bed. The bedroom door flew out of Uncle Quentin's hand and slammed itself shut so violently that a vase leapt off a nearby shelf.

'This wretched gale,' said Uncle Quentin fiercely. 'I've never known one like it in all the time we've lived in this house.'

'It'll blow itself out, dear,' said Aunt Fanny soothingly. 'Probably by the time the morning comes it'll be quite calm.'

Go to **21**.

30

George dozed fitfully for a while, woken over and over again by the sound of the wind rising to a scream. Timmy kept disturbing her too, with his restless pacing about the room, and she began to be alarmed that he would knock over some of her father's precious test-tubes and bottles. In the end she could bear it no longer. She got up and went through to the dining-room, where her parents were trying to sleep.

'Mother!' she whispered.

'What is it, George?' said her mother irritably.

'Mother, I'm very worried about Timmy. He won't settle down, the storm is making him very restless, and I'm afraid he might knock one of the bottles or test-tubes over. I really do think we should go in the sitting-room with the boys.'

Go to **22**.

31

If you've arrived from **43**, *score* ◁ .

George gave her father a glare and scrambled into

the car. Though she looked cross, she didn't look as sad at parting with Timmy as the others had expected. The car drove away from Kirrin Cottage with the children waving at their aunt and uncle. Their spirits rose as they thought of Sooty and Smuggler's Top. George sat in silence as the car drove on. The car went over a hill and sped down to the bottom. When they got there George leaned forward and touched the driver's arm.

'Would you please stop a moment? We have to pick somebody up here.'

The driver, rather surprised, stopped. George opened the car door and gave a loud whistle.

Something shot out of the hedge and hurled itself joyfully into the car. It was Timmy! The children were all delighted to see him.

'On to Smuggler's Top,' said Dick, as the car moved forward. 'I wonder if we shall have any adventures there!'

Go to **26**.

32

'How many people have been sucked down into the marsh and never seen again?' Dick asked the driver.

'Quite a few,' he replied. 'They do say there's one or two winding paths that go to the hill from the mainland that were used before the road was built. But unless you know every inch of them you're off them in a trice, and sinking into the mud.'

'It's horrible to think of people being sucked into the mud,' said Anne as the car moved slowly along the road. 'Don't let's talk about it any more. Can we see Castaway Hill yet?'

'Yes. There it is looming up out of the mist,' said the driver. 'Strange-looking place, isn't it?'

They all gazed in silence. Out of the slowly moving mists rose a tall, steep hill, whose rocky sides were as sheer as cliffs. It was covered with buildings which even at that distance looked old and interesting.

'That must be Smuggler's Top, right at the summit,' said Julian, pointing. 'Look at the tower it has! What a wonderful view you'd get from it.'

Go to **41**.

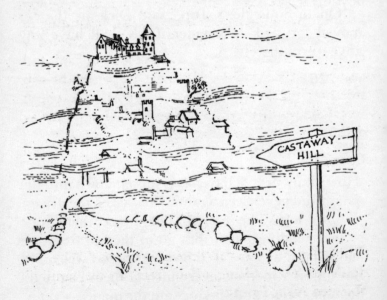

32

33

Julian stood at the window watching the ash tree bending in the wind. Then suddenly the wind dropped, and the tree slowly straightened up. Julian watched it for a little while longer, then got back into bed.

'I thought the ash tree was going to fall on the house!' he said to Dick, 'but I think it'll be all right now.'

Dick turned out the bedside light and the two boys lay in the dark, listening to the wind screaming around the old house. Julian was just beginning to feel drowsy after his long day when he heard a creaking, groaning noise. He got out of bed and rushed to the window. He expected to see the ash tree bending again, but instead he saw the beech tree that grew just beside it swaying violently. It was definitely falling towards the house!

Go to **27**.

34

'But Quentin – you can't possibly do that! Why, we don't know anything about him or his family!' objected Aunt Fanny.

'His boy goes to the same school as Julian and Dick, and I know Lenoir is a remarkable, clever fellow,' said Uncle Quentin, as if that was all that mattered. 'I'll telephone him now.'

He went out of the room to use the telephone in his study.

The children had just finished their breakfast when Uncle Quentin called to them.

'Come here, you four, please. I want to talk to you.'

Go to **25**.

35

There was a lot of giggling and scuffling as the children closed the door. Then Uncle Quentin's footsteps were heard on the stairs, and the five fled silently to their rooms.

The gale still roared. Uncle Quentin and Aunt Fanny came up to bed. The bedroom door flew out of Uncle Quentin's hand and slammed itself shut so violently that a vase leapt off a nearby shelf.

Uncle Quentin leapt too. 'This wretched gale,' he said fiercely. 'I've never known one like it in all the time we've been here.'

'It'll blow itself out soon, dear,' said Aunt Fanny soothingly. 'Probably by the time morning comes it'll be quite calm.'

Go to **21**.

Soon George got up and went into the boys' room, where Julian and Dick were hastily packing.

'Which road do we take to Smuggler's Top, Julian?' she asked.

'The coast road, I think,' replied Julian. 'Why?'

'Oh, I just wondered,' said George. Whistling to Timmy, she went off downstairs, and the others didn't see her for some time. When she came back she looked more cheerful, but Timmy wasn't with her.

'Where's Timmy?' asked Julian in surprise.

'Oh, he's out somewhere,' answered George. 'By the way, I've decided I shall come with you.' For some reason she didn't look Julian in the eye as she spoke.

They had just finished packing when the hired car arrived.

'Right,' said Uncle Quentin. 'In you get.'

'I haven't said goodbye to Timmy,' objected George.

'Never mind about saying goodbye to your dog,' said her father. 'Now, do as you're told and get into the car!'

George glared at her father. 'I'm going to say goodbye to Timmy!'

Uncle Quentin looked furious. 'Georgina, obey me at once!'

*If you think George obeys her father, go to **31**.*
*If you think she doesn't, go to **43**.*

'The tree has crashed through the attic, smashed the roof in and wrecked the girls' bedroom,' said Uncle Quentin. 'A big branch has penetrated the boys' room too, but not badly. The girls' room is ruined. They would have been killed if they'd been in their beds.'

Everyone was silent. It was an awful thought that George and Anne had had such a narrow escape.

'I think some hot cocoa would do us all good,' said Aunt Fanny. 'I'll go and make some. Quentin, see if the fire is still alight in your study. We need a little warmth!'

They all drank their cocoa, huddled around the fire in the study. It was no use going back up to bed, so they had to decide where everyone was to sleep for what remained of the night. Aunt Fanny found camp-beds and put them in the study for the girls, and piled blankets and pillows on the sitting-room floor for the boys.

'Can't we all sleep together, Aunt Fanny?' begged Anne. 'It would be much more fun!'

'No,' said her aunt. 'You've had a long day, and not much sleep so far. You'd all chatter and keep each other awake. The boys must go in the sitting-room.'

'Oh, please, Mother,' said George. 'Please let us all be together.'

If you think Aunt Fanny gives in, go to **22**.
If you think she insists they sleep in separate rooms, go to **42**.

38

They got into the car again, Timmy clambering over legs and feet to a comfortable place on George's lap. After a while Anne fell asleep, and the others all felt drowsy after their broken night.

Some time later the driver spoke to Julian.

'We're just coming to the marsh now, so it won't be long before we get to Castaway.'

Julian woke Anne, and they all sat up and peered eagerly out of the windows. However, all they could see was mist and a few yards of the road ahead, raised above the surrounding marsh. From time to time they caught a glimpse of flat boggy land stretching away on either side. It all looked very dreary.

Go to **32**.

39

George wriggled herself into a more comfortable position and decided to stay in bed. Unfortunately, Julian and Dick were thinking that one of the girls might shut the bathroom door, so nobody got up to close it!

Very soon Uncle Quentin's voice roared up the stairs, louder than the gale.

'Shut that door, one of you! How can I work with that noise going on?'

All four children jumped out of bed like a shot.

Timmy leapt off George's bed. Everyone fell over him as they rushed to the bathroom door.

Go to **35**.

40

If you've arrived from **28**, *score* ⌣.

The letter turned out to be from Mr Lenoir. Uncle Quentin read it through, and then looked at the children.

'This is what he says,' Uncle Quentin told them. ' "It is most kind of you to suggest my coming to stay with you and bringing my son Pierre. Allow me to extend hospitality to you and your children also. I do not know how many you have, but all are welcome here in this big house. Pierre will be glad of company, and so will his sister Mary." '

Uncle Quentin looked triumphantly at his wife.

'There you are! I call that a most generous invitation! It couldn't have come at a better time. We'll pack the children off to this fellow's house!'

Go to **34**.

41

As they neared Castaway Hill the road began to slope upwards.

'I believe we go through a big archway,' said the driver. 'It's where the city gate once was. The whole town is surrounded by a wall, which is wide enough to walk on, and if you start at a certain place and walk long enough, you'll come back to the place you started at!'

All the children made up their minds to do this without fail. What a view there would be, if they chose a fine day.

They came to a sort of courtyard in front of the town walls, and the driver stopped.

'My instructions say go through an archway,' he said, 'but there are *two* archways here. Which one is it, I wonder?'

They had left the mist behind as they came up the hill, and the sun shone on the old cobbled yard and the grey stone of the wall. The two arches looked very similar. They had rounded tops and were built of the same hard grey stone as the wall, softened by patches of orange lichen here and there. Through the left-hand arch they could see the road running between old, weathered houses. Through the right-hand arch they could see what looked like another courtyard.

'Which way should we go?' said Dick. 'Left or right?'

If you think they should take the left-hand arch, go to **47**.
If you think they should take the right-hand arch, go to **53**.

42

'No,' said Aunt Fanny. 'As I said, you'll talk for most of what's left of the night if I put you all in the same room. Now off you go, boys, to the sitting-room, and George and Anne, you settle down here. Good night!'

Anne and George made themselves as comfortable as they could, but the noise of the storm kept them awake. It made Timmy restless too. Instead of curling up happily at George's feet, he paced restlessly around the study, sniffing at the strange bottles that Uncle Quentin used for his experiments.

Go to **30**.

43

George suddenly dashed off round the side of the house.

'George!' shouted her father. 'Come back here at once!'

But it was too late. George had vanished.

Uncle Quentin stood by the car, fuming and looking at his watch. 'If she doesn't come back soon you'll be late,' he said. 'I've arranged for you all to have lunch at an inn on the way.'

They all waited by the car, Uncle Quentin getting crosser and crosser. Eventually George reappeared, looking defiant.

'If you weren't going away I should certainly punish you for your disobedience, George!' said her father. 'Now, get into the car. You've kept everyone waiting quite long enough.'

Go to **31**.

The children all passed through the opening into the secret passage. Sooty came last and did something that shut the opening and slid the first panel back into its place again. Then he switched on a small torch, because it was pitch dark in the passage, and they could see that it was built of stone. It was so narrow that two people could not have passed one another unless they were as thin as rakes. Sooty handed his torch to Julian, who was in front.

'Keep straight on until you come to some stone steps,' he said. 'Go up them, turn to the right at the top, and keep straight on until you come to a blank wall, then I'll tell you what to do.'

They moved along the passage as far as the steps Sooty had mentioned.

'Don't make a row,' said Sooty. 'We're passing the dining-room now. There's a way into this passage from there, too.'

They walked on until Julian came to the blank wall.

Go to **48**.

Go to **48**.

45

'My stepfather sometimes seems very secretive,' said Sooty, 'but I don't think he's a smuggler.'

'What do you mean, secretive?' asked Julian.

'Well, strange men come here at night, and sometimes I've seen lights shining from our tower,' Sooty replied, 'but I don't think they're smuggling. We have got one man living in Castaway, though, who everyone knows is a smuggler. He's called Barling. He's very rich. The police are suspicious of him, but they can never prove anything.'

He stopped speaking and held up his hand. The buzzer had sounded. Someone was coming down the passage!

'Perhaps it's your stepfather,' said George in alarm.

'It may be his manservant, Block, coming to tell us tea is ready,' said Sooty, opening the door. 'Quick, shut Timmy in the cupboard!'

If you think it's Mr Lenoir in the passage, go to **57**.
If you think it's Block, the manservant, go to **63**.

46

The driver saw George waving and stopped the car.

'What is it?' he asked. 'Have you forgotten something?'

'No,' said George, 'but I'm not staying here because they won't have my dog. You'll have to take us back to Kirrin with you.'

The driver looked a bit doubtful. 'What will your parents say if you appear on their doorstep again?' he asked.

'I'll worry about that when I get home,' said George firmly.

'All right, then, it's up to you,' said the driver,

and George jumped in the back with Timmy.

The others chased down the drive after the car, but it was no good. It disappeared through the gates back into the town.

Go to **49**.

47

If you've arrived from **50**, *score* ⤲ ⤲ ⤲.

'It must be the left-hand arch,' said George. 'The road is going uphill, and we know Smuggler's Top is at the summit, so it makes sense to keep going up, doesn't it?'

The car moved forwards through the arch and up the winding street. It was lined on either side with old houses and shops that had diamond-paned windows and stout wooden doors. The street was cobbled, which made the car bounce around a great deal.

At last they came to a pair of wrought-iron gates. The driver hooted his horn, and a man appeared and opened them. They swept into a steep drive and at last stopped before Smuggler's Top.

Go to **55**.

48

'Shine your torch up to where the roof of the passage meets the wall, Julian,' said Sooty. 'You'll see an iron handle there. Pull down on it hard.'

Julian did as Sooty said, and quite suddenly the stone in the middle of the wall slid forwards and sideways, leaving a gaping hole.

'Go on, Julian,' said Sooty. 'You'll find you're in a cupboard in my bedroom.'

One by one they all followed Julian through the hole, round Sooty's clothes and into his room. Sooty brought up the rear.

'We're safe here in my room,' he said. 'Mary's room is just next door, and we're quite separate from the rest of the house. Look!'

He opened the door and showed the others what he meant. There was one room, next to his, which was Mary's, and beyond stretched a stone-floored passage. At the end of it a big window let in the light. There was a door there, a great oak one, which was closed.

Go to **51**.

49

Julian, Dick and Anne stood on the drive and looked at each other.

'I don't know what Uncle Quentin will say when George arrives home again,' said Julian.

'He'll be absolutely furious,' said Dick. 'Anyway, there isn't a room for her to sleep in. She'll be sent back to school, and she won't like that very much!'

'I don't think George minds about anyone but Timmy,' said Anne rather sadly. She felt a bit hurt that George was more concerned about Timmy than about her cousins.

Sooty and Mary came running up to join them. 'Has your sister gone?' asked Sooty.

Go to **54**.

50

It was a narrow, cobbled street, with room for only one car at a time. Looking out of the window, George realised that if she put her hand out she could touch the wall, it was so close to her.

It was very dark, almost like a tunnel, and looking up they could see that houses overhung the street and cut out nearly all the light. Anne gave a sudden shiver. Castaway looked quite exciting in the sunshine, but the gloomy street felt rather sinister.

The street sloped upwards quite sharply, and at the top they went under another arch, formed by two houses that had been built out over the road. The driver looked left and right. The road they were now in was much wider, with shops on either side of it. To the right they could see the road disappearing up the hill, but to the left it sloped down to another arch, only a few metres away.

The driver turned left, and a moment later they bounced through the arch and found themselves in the little courtyard with high blank walls.

'Goodness,' said Julian. 'We're back where we started from!'

On the other side of the courtyard they could see the arch that led out of the walled town, and soon they were back outside the walls, once more facing the two arches.

Go to **47**.

51

'I've got a way of knowing when anyone opens that door,' said Sooty proudly. 'Look!'

He ran along the passage and opened the door at the end. Immediately a low buzzing noise sounded somewhere in his room. Sooty shut the door and ran back.

'I rigged it up so that I would always know when someone was coming,' he said.

Anne had gone to the window to look at the view.

'Goodness!' she exclaimed. 'How steep it is. Can you see the sea if there's no mist?'

'Oh, yes,' replied Sooty. 'Though people do say it's getting further and further back. Apparently there's some sort of scheme afoot to drain the marsh and use the land for farming.'

'The marsh looks as if it would be a good place for smugglers,' said Dick. 'Are there any round here?'

Go to **45**.

52

If you've arrived from **58**, *score* ◁.

Sooty opened the door just enough for him to see into the room. It was empty, but the radio was on!

'Come on,' he said. 'There's no one here. It was the radio we could hear. We'll take the secret passage to my bedroom.'

The children looked at each other. A secret passage sounded thrilling! Sooty went to one of the oak panels that covered the walls of the study and pressed it in a certain place. It slid aside softly. Sooty put in his hand and pulled something. A much larger panel below slid into the wall and left an opening big enough for the children to get through.

'Come on,' said Sooty. 'Don't make a noise.'

Go to **44**.

53

'Let's try the right-hand arch,' said Julian. 'I'm sure it's that one.'

The car moved forwards through the archway and into the other courtyard. It was cobbled, like the one they had just left, and was surrounded by blank walls. Craning their necks, the children could see that the walls were the backs of houses that had their front doors on streets higher up the hill. In one corner of the courtyard was another arch. It was only just wide enough to get the car through, and the driver had to go very slowly.

'Goodness!' exclaimed Anne as they came through the arch. 'How strange!'

Go to **56**.

'Yes,' said Julian. 'She's gone back with the driver.'

'Why on earth didn't she stay here?' asked Sooty. 'All I said was that my stepfather didn't allow dogs at Smuggler's Top.'

'You don't know how George feels about Timmy,' said Dick. 'She's absolutely devoted to him – he's almost like a human being as far as she's concerned.'

Just then the car suddenly appeared on the drive again! They all ran to meet it.

'George! George!' shouted Dick. 'Have you changed your mind and decided to stay?'

'No,' said George, getting out of the car. 'I left my suitcase here, and it's got all my clothes in it.'

Sooty stepped forwards. 'George, please stay,' he said. 'I'm sure we can find some way of hiding your dog.'

George thought for a moment. She really hated the idea of going back to Kirrin without the others, and she knew how angry her father would be.

'*Please* stay,' said Sooty again.

'All right,' she said reluctantly. 'I will.'

'Right,' said Sooty. 'Come on!'

He opened a small door in the wall of the house and ushered them all inside. They found themselves in a dark passage.

Go to **64**.

They got out of the car, feeling rather shy. The big old house seemed to frown down at them. It was built of brick and timber, and the front door was as massive as that of a castle. The house's one tower stood sturdily at the east side, with windows all the way around it, and a pointed roof.

Dick rang the bell. They waited for a minute, then there was the sound of running feet, and the door opened. Beyond it stood two children, one a boy of Dick's age, and the other a girl who seemed to be about Anne's age.

'Here you are at last!' said the boy. 'I thought you were never coming!'

'This is Sooty,' Dick said to George and Anne. They stared at him. He certainly was very dark, with black hair and eyebrows, dark eyes and brown skin. In contrast, the girl was fair, with blue eyes.

'This is Mary, my sister,' said Sooty, smiling all over his face. Then suddenly he stopped smiling and looked serious. 'That's not your dog, is it?' he asked, pointing at Timmy, who had got out of the car with the others.

'Yes, it is,' answered George. 'He's mine, and I never go anywhere without him!'

'My stepfather won't have dogs at Smuggler's Top,' said Sooty, looking worried.

'I thought maybe we'd be able to hide him some-where,' George replied crossly. 'However, if that's how you feel, Timmy and I will go back home with the car.'

She turned and ran back to where the driver was starting to turn the car round. Timmy followed her.

'Hey – wait for me!' she called.

If you think George and Timmy go off in the car, go to **46**.
If you think they don't, go to **61**.

56

They were in yet another courtyard! It was much bigger than the one they had come from, and there were old wooden doors in places around the walls. Steep flights of steps ran down into it here and there. They led up to the back doors of houses on the hill.

'I expect people used to have coal and things like that delivered here,' said Julian, 'so that the horses didn't have to pull heavy loads up the steep roads.'

There was another arch in the centre of the wall to their right, and the driver nosed the car through it and on to the road that lay beyond.

Go to **50**.

57

Sooty went out into the passage, closing the door behind him in case the others didn't get Timmy into the cupboard quickly enough. Coming down the passage was his stepfather.

'Oh, there you are, Pierre,' said Mr Lenoir. 'I was wondering where you'd got to. Your mother and I can't understand why you haven't brought your friends down to be introduced to us yet. We heard them arrive quite some time ago.'

'I'm sorry, Father,' said Pierre. 'I was so pleased to see them that I rushed them up here without thinking.'

'I will not tolerate bad manners, Pierre,' said his stepfather. 'Now, take me to meet your friends.'

Sooty turned back towards his room, hoping that the others had got Timmy hidden!

Go to **60**.

58

'Oh, no, please don't open the door,' begged George. 'Supposing your stepfather sees Timmy!'

'All right,' said Sooty. 'We'll wait until we're sure the room is empty.'

They had to wait a very long time. Timmy got impatient at having to sit still for so long, and gave one or two tiny whimpers. George hushed him quickly.

'Shall we play a game?' said Dick. 'I Spy, or something?'

'You'll have to do it very, very quietly,' warned Sooty. 'These doors are thick, but my stepfather's hearing is very sharp.'

Speaking in whispers, they played I Spy for a while. It wasn't a very good game because the passage was dark and they couldn't see much, but it passed the time.

Suddenly Sooty held up his hand for silence.

'I'm going to have a look,' he whispered.

Go to **52**.

59

If you've arrived from **65**, *score* ◡◠ ◡◠.

'About a year,' said Sooty. 'He suddenly appeared one day. Even Mother didn't know he was coming. I suppose my stepfather was expecting him, but he didn't say anything to my mother. She seemed very surprised.'

'Is your stepfather Mary's stepfather too?' asked Anne.

'No,' replied Sooty. 'Mary and I are half brother and sister. We have the same mother, but my stepfather is Mary's real father.'

'It's rather muddled,' said Anne.

'Don't worry about it,' said Sooty. 'Come on – we'd better go downstairs. By the way, my step-father often seems very affable, always laughing and joking, but he's got a very quick temper. My mother's quite different. She's very quiet and shy. Mary is like her.'

Leaving Timmy shut in the cupboard in case Block came up and started snooping, they all went to see Mr Lenoir.

Go to **62**.

Just as Sooty was about to open his bedroom door, the door at the end of the passage opened again and a man in a white jacket and black trousers came towards Sooty and his stepfather.

'You are wanted on the telephone, sir,' he said to Mr Lenoir in a flat, monotonous voice.

'Very well, Block,' said Mr Lenoir. 'I'll come straight down. You make sure that Pierre's friends come to my study as soon as possible. I want to meet them.' He turned and went back through the door at the end of the passage.

'Your friends are in your room?' Block asked Sooty.

Sooty nodded, and opened the door of his bedroom.

Go to **65**.

61

Sooty stared after George.

'Come back, stupid!' he yelled. 'We'll think of something to do about your dog!'

He ran down the steps that led to the front door and tore after George. The others followed. Mary went too, shutting the big front door behind her.

There was a small door in the wall just where George was standing. The driver hadn't seen her waving at him, and, as they watched, the car slid away down the drive. Sooty caught hold of George and pushed her through the door, then held it open for the others.

They found themselves in a dark passage.

Go to **64**.

62

On the other side of the big oak door was a great flight of wide, shallow stairs. At the bottom of the stairs was a large hall. Sooty opened a door on the right and ushered the others into his stepfather's study.

'Here they all are,' he said. 'Sorry I rushed them off to my bedroom like that, Father, but I was so excited to see them all!'

Mr Lenoir was sitting behind his desk. He was a neat, clever-looking man with fair hair and blue eyes. He smiled a great deal, but only with his mouth, not with his eyes.

The four of them shook hands with Mr Lenoir, and then Sooty introduced them to his mother, who was so small and frail-looking she seemed lost in her big armchair by the window.

'I hope you'll all enjoy yourselves while you're staying with us,' said Mrs Lenoir. 'I was sorry to hear about the damage to your house.'

She was interrupted by Mr Lenoir, who spoke to Julian.

'I hope your uncle will come and fetch you when you go home, because I would like to talk to him. We've been doing the same kinds of experiment, but he is further ahead than I am.'

'I think we'd better ask the children where they'd like to have their meals,' said Mrs Lenoir in her soft voice. 'Would you like to have them in the play-room, which is next door to Mary's bedroom, or in the dining-room with us?'

If you think they should choose the dining-room, go to **69**.
If you think they should have their meals in the playroom, go to **75**.

63

Coming down the passage was a man in a white coat and black trousers. He had a strange, closed face.

'Hello, Block!' said Sooty. He turned to the others. 'Block is my stepfather's manservant. By the way, he's stone deaf, but don't think you can say

what you like in front of him, because he often seems to sense what's being said.'

'Your stepfather and your mother wonder why you have not brought your friends down to meet them yet,' said Block in a flat, monotonous voice. 'Why did you rush up here like this?'

'Oh, I was so pleased to see them I didn't think about my parents,' replied Sooty. 'We'll be down in a minute, Block.'

Block left the room without another word.

'I don't like him,' said Anne. 'Has he been with you long?'

Go to **59**.

64

If you've arrived from **54**, *score* ⌒ ⌒.

There was a door at the other end of the passage.

'Wait here a minute and I'll see if the coast is clear,' said Sooty. 'I know my stepfather is in, and I tell you, if he sees that dog he'll pack you all off back to Kirrin. I don't want him to do that because I can't tell you how I've looked forward to having you all!'

He grinned at them, and even George thought how nice he was, even though she hadn't taken to him at first. They all felt a bit scared of Mr Lenoir, though. He sounded rather fierce!

Sooty tiptoed to the door at the end of the passage and listened.

'I can hear voices in the study,' he said. 'We'll have to wait until it's empty.'

They waited for what seemed ages, while the buzz of voices went on and on.

'Shall I have a look and see if there's really someone in there?' whispered Sooty.

'No!' hissed George.

'Yes, do,' said Julian, both at the same time.

If you think Sooty should open the door, go to **52**.
If you think he shouldn't, go to **58**.

65

'This is Block, my stepfather's manservant,' said Sooty to the others. 'He's stone deaf, but don't think you can say what you like in front of him, because he often seems to sense what is being said.'

'Mr Lenoir would like to see you downstairs in his study immediately,' said Block in his strange, flat voice. 'Don't keep him waiting.'

He stalked out of the room, and a moment later they heard the buzzer sound, showing that Block had gone through the door at the end of the passage.

'I don't think I like him,' said Anne. 'Has he been here long?'

Go to **59**.

66

Rather scared, Julian, Dick, Anne and George hurried from the room, followed by Sooty and Mary. Sooty was grinning as he shut the door.

'I didn't promise!' he said. 'He wanted to take all our fun away. This place isn't any good if you don't explore it.'

'What are catacombs?' asked Anne.

'Winding, secret tunnels in the hill,' said Sooty. 'You can get lost in them easily, and never get out again.'

'Who would use them, I wonder?' said George.

'Smugglers, I expect,' replied Julian. 'The catacombs would be a good place to hide themselves and their goods. According to Sooty there still *is* a smuggler living in Castaway. What did you say his name was?'

'Barling,' said Sooty. 'Now come upstairs and I'll show you your rooms before tea.'

Go to **73**.

67

At breakfast the next morning the children couldn't discuss how they were going to get Timmy out of the house for a walk because Block was in and out of the playroom, bringing toast and large plates of bacon and eggs.

'I must say your mother is a jolly good cook, Sooty,' said Dick with his mouth full.

'She doesn't do the cooking, silly,' said Sooty. 'We have a cook. Her name is Sarah.'

'Goodness,' said Anne. 'Your stepfather must be

quite well off if he can afford to have a manservant *and* a cook.'

'Yes, I think he is,' said Sooty. 'We're very lucky really.'

After breakfast George released Timmy from his hiding-place in Sooty's cupboard, and they all went into Mary's room.

'What does this room have to do with Timmy's walk?' asked George.

'I'll show you,' replied Sooty with a grin.

Go to **70**.

68

After tea they unpacked, and that evening they played cards with Sooty and Mary in the playroom. After their broken night and long journey all four of them were very sleepy, so they decided to go to bed early.

'What about Timmy?' George asked Sooty. 'He always sleeps on my bed.'

'That's easy,' Sooty told her. 'Just wait until everyone's gone to bed, and then come along to my room and I'll let him out of the cupboard and you can take him over to your room. Then you can bring him back in the morning before anyone else is up.'

George got ready for bed and waited until the house was quiet. Then she opened her bedroom door and peered out cautiously. All the doors around the landing were closed, so she ran quietly across to the oak door into the passage. Sooty heard the buzzer go as George opened the door, and he fetched Timmy from his hiding-place just as George came through his bedroom door.

'Bring him back before half-past six, won't you?' said Sooty. 'That's when Block gets up, and we don't want him to see you.'

George and Timmy ran back down the passage, slipped through the oak door and began to cross the landing. Suddenly George stopped, frozen with horror. She could hear someone coming! What could she do? She wondered whether to make a dash for her room or to try to hide.

If you think she should make a dash for her room, go to **76**.
If you think she should hide, go to **81**.

69

If you've arrived from **75**, *score* ⌢.

At that moment the door opened and Block came in.

'Tea is ready,' he announced.

'Ah, Block,' said Mr Lenoir, turning to face him. 'Pierre, Mary and our visitors will be having all their meals in the playroom. I don't care for noisy talk at the table, so I've decided they will eat upstairs.'

'Very good, sir,' said Block, and he stalked out of the room.

'Well, off you go and have tea,' said Mrs Lenoir.

'By the way, Pierre,' said Mr Lenoir, 'I forbid you to wander about in the catacombs under this hill, nor are you to play about on the city wall. I will not have you taking risks now you have friends here. Will you promise not to disobey me?'

'I don't play about on the city wall, Father,' protested Sooty. 'I don't take risks, either.'

'Don't argue with me!' snapped his stepfather, suddenly losing his temper. 'Now go and have tea!'

Go to **66**.

70

Sooty began to move the furniture in the room to the sides. The others watched in surprise for a minute, then helped him.

'What's the idea of the furniture removal?' asked Dick, struggling with a heavy chest.

'We've got to get the carpet up,' replied Sooty. 'There's a trapdoor underneath it.'

The others looked at each other. A trapdoor! It sounded very exciting.

They dragged the heavy carpet back until they could see the trapdoor. It was let flat into the floor, with a ring handle to pull it up.

'Mary, go down to the end of the passage and check that no one is coming, will you?' said Sooty.

Mary ran to the door at the end of the passage. She was back in seconds.

'I can hear someone coming up the stairs!' she said.

'It's probably Block,' suggested Julian.

*If you think it's Block who's coming, go to **77**.*
*If not, go to **84**.*

71

*If you've arrived from **74**, score* ⚮ ⚮.

Sooty switched on his torch, and the children gave a gasp. The trapdoor led down to a pit far below the foundations of the house.

'How in the world will we get Timmy down there?' asked George. 'Or get down there ourselves, for that matter? I'm not going to jump down, that's certain!'

Sooty laughed. 'You won't have to,' he said. 'Look here.' He opened a cupboard and pulled something down from one of the shelves. He held it up, and the children could see that it was a rope ladder, fine but very strong. 'There you are! We can all get down by that,' he said.

'Timmy can't,' said George at once. 'How on earth are we going to get him into that pit?'

*Go to **79**.*

72

*If you've arrived from **82**, score* ⚮ ⚮.

'I think we'd better try the laundry basket,' said

George. 'It sounds a safer way of doing things.'

'It's in the kitchen,' said Sooty. 'I'll go and get it.'

He was gone only for a short time, and when he came back he was carrying a large wicker laundry hamper on his head.

'Good,' said Julian. 'How did you get it? Did anyone mind?'

'Didn't ask them,' said Sooty with a grin. 'There was no one there. Block's with Father, and Sarah's gone shopping. I can always put it back if any awkward questions are asked.'

He put down the basket and opened the lid. Timmy was made to get inside and lie down. He was surprised, and gave a little bark, but George put her hand over his mouth.

'Sh! You mustn't make a noise, Timmy,' she said. 'I know this is all rather strange, but you're going to have a marvellous walk soon.'

Then she shut the lid on him.

Go to **83**.

73

Sooty showed them two rooms next to each other, on the opposite side of the big staircase from his bedroom and Mary's. Both rooms had a marvellous view over the roofs and towers of Castaway Hill, and they also had a remarkably good view of Mr Barling's house.

George liked her room but she was worried about being so far away from Timmy.

'We'll have to arrange to feed and exercise Timmy, you know,' she said to Sooty. 'Oh, I do hope he'll be all right.'

'He'll be fine,' replied Sooty. 'I'll give him the free run of that narrow passage we came up to my bedroom by, and I'll raid the larder at night for scraps to feed him on. I'll show you a way we can smuggle him into the town for exercise, too.'

Go to **68**.

74

The children all breathed a sigh of relief as the door closed behind Mr Lenoir, but nobody spoke until they heard the faint sound of the warning buzzer in Sooty's room, which told them that Mr Lenoir had gone back through the oak door.

'Phew,' said Dick, getting to his feet. 'That was a near thing!'

George was fumbling with the door of the wardrobe. She pulled it open, and out jumped Timmy!

'I wondered what you'd done with Timmy,' said Mary. 'I was scared Father would come in here and find him.'

'He was very good,' said George, making a fuss of the big dog. 'He never made a sound.'

'Right,' said Sooty. 'Lock the door, Dick, and we'll try again.'

He bent down and pulled the carpet back again, and then hauled up the trapdoor. They all peered down, but it was pitch black and they could see nothing.

'Are there steps down?' asked Julian.

'No,' said Sooty, reaching for a big torch he had brought from his room. He saw Julian looking at the torch and grinned. 'It's all right, Julian, this really is mine and not Father's. Now look!'

Go to **71**.

75

The children looked at each other. They weren't sure that they wanted to have meals with the grown-ups, but thought it might be rude to refuse.

'The dining-room, please,' said Julian. 'It's nice of you to ask us.'

George, Dick and Anne exchanged horrified glances. None of them liked the look of Mr Lenoir!

'We usually have lunch at about one o'clock,' went on Mrs Lenoir, 'and breakfast is at half-past eight.'

Mr Lenoir interrupted her again. 'I think I'd like the children to have all their meals in the playroom,' he said. 'As you know, my dear, I don't like noise at meals. It distracts me when I'm trying to think about my work. I shall tell Block to serve them upstairs.'

'Very well, Father,' said Sooty meekly, but the others could see him give a broad wink.

Go to **69**.

If you've arrived from **78**, *score* ◁ ◁ .

George decided to make a dash for her room.

'Come on, Timmy,' she hissed. 'Run!'

Just as she reached the bedroom door, somebody tapped George on the shoulder. George almost jumped out of her skin, then a familiar voice whispered her name. 'George! Are you all right?'

It was Julian. 'I thought I'd come and check that Timmy was none the worse for his spell in hiding,' he explained.

'Well, you nearly made me die of fright, tapping me on the shoulder!' hissed George crossly.

'Sorry, old thing,' said Julian. 'I'll go back to bed and leave you in peace now.'

He vanished into his bedroom, and George climbed thankfully into bed, with Timmy curled up in his usual place by her feet.

Go to **67**.

'Go back and look, Mary,' said Sooty. 'See who it is, then come and tell us.'

Mary sped off along the passage again and opened the oak door a crack. She could see Block coming up the stairs, carrying two of Mr Lenoir's suits over his arm. He didn't seem to notice Mary, but turned towards the Lenoirs' bedroom. Mary ran back to the others.

'It's all right,' she reported. 'It was only Block with some of Father's suits – I expect he's been brushing them.'

Sooty locked the door of Mary's bedroom then pulled up the trapdoor. They all peered down but they could see nothing. It was pitch black.

'Are there steps down?' asked Julian.

'No,' said Sooty, reaching for a big torch he had brought with him. 'Look!'

Go to **71**.

78

It was Block! It seemed to George that he was staring straight at her, but after what seemed like hours he moved, and she heard his steps going away. She knew he was going downstairs because the wooden staircase creaked loudly whenever someone went up or down.

George waited a long time before she dared get off the seat. Her knees were trembling and the palms of her hands were clammy. At last she decided to risk it, so she climbed down, followed by Timmy. The two of them had started back to George's room when Timmy suddenly gave a tiny growl.

'What is it, Timmy? What's the matter?' whispered George.

A moment later she knew why Timmy had growled. She could hear footsteps again!

Go to **76**.

George looked at Timmy, and then back at the pit.
She thought of trying to climb down the rope ladder
with Timmy under her arm, but knew at once that it
wouldn't work. He was much too big and heavy.

'I know what we'll do!' said Mary.

'I've got an idea,' said Dick at the same time.

'What do you think we should do, Mary?' asked
George.

'We could get the big laundry hamper, put
Timmy in it and then tie a rope to it. Then we could
lower him into the pit.'

George turned to Dick. 'What's your idea?' she
asked.

'We could make a sling from a rug or something,
attach a rope to it, and then lower him down like
that,' replied Dick.

'Which would be best, George?' asked Sooty.

*If you think they should use the laundry hamper, go
to* **72**.

If you think they should make a sling, go to **86**.

80

He stood on the threshold looking at the children.
They were all sitting on the floor, playing jacks. The
carpet was back in place, and George was leaning
on the door of Mary's wardrobe.

'What have you done with all the furniture?'

asked Mr Lenoir. 'Why is it pushed against the walls like that?'

'We wanted plenty of room to play jacks, Father,' said Sooty. 'The table in here is too small for all of us to play on, so we decided to use the floor.'

Mr Lenoir didn't really listen to Sooty's explanation. He looked all around the room as if searching for something, then glared at them all.

'The big torch is missing from my desk,' he said. 'Have any of you seen it?'

'No, Mr Lenoir, we haven't,' replied Julian. 'We haven't been anywhere near your study this morning.'

'Are you sure?' asked Mr Lenoir.

'Quite sure,' said Julian a little stiffly. He didn't like the feeling that Mr Lenoir thought he was lying.

'Well, if I find one of you has taken it, it'll be the worse for you,' said Mr Lenoir, and he stormed out.

Go to **74**.

81

George looked around the landing. At the head of the stairs was a large window with a wide, cushioned window seat. It was hung with heavy velvet curtains. Quickly she pushed Timmy up on to the seat, then she jumped up herself and pulled the curtains. The sound of footsteps came nearer and nearer. George put one hand on Timmy's head, to stop him growling, and held her breath. Her heart was thumping so loudly that she felt sure it could be heard all over the house. The footsteps stopped, and she could hear someone breathing on the other side of the curtains.

In her haste George hadn't quite closed the curtains, and now she put her eye to the gap. She could just make out a figure standing with his back to her. As she watched, he turned round so that she could see his face.

Go to **78**.

82

'Right,' said George. 'Now, we'd better see if this is going to work before we try to lower Timmy into that pit. If I climb on the chest of drawers, Julian, and you pass me the rope, I'll try lifting Timmy up. I won't be able to lift him very far, but at least we'll be able to see if the sling is safe.'

Julian picked up the rope while George scrambled on to the chest of drawers. She took hold of the rope in both hands and tried to lift Timmy up, but it was no use. Timmy tipped forwards and the sling slipped over his back legs. She tried again a couple of times, but the same thing happened each time.

'It's no good,' said George. 'This isn't going to work. He'll fall out and hurt himself.' She jumped down to the floor.

'What shall we do?' said Dick.

Go to **72**.

83

They tied the rope firmly around the hamper, then
Sooty let himself down into the hole, holding his
torch between his teeth. Down and down he went,
until at last he stood safely on the bottom. His voice
floated up to the others. It sounded strange and far
away.

'Come on! Lower Timmy down!'

The laundry hamper, feeling extraordinarily
heavy now, was pushed to the edge of the hole. Then
down it went, knocking against the sides here and
there. Timmy growled. He didn't like this game!
Finally the basket landed at the bottom with a slight
bump, and Sooty lifted the lid. Timmy leapt out,
barking, but the bark sounded very small and dis-
tant to the watchers at the top.

'Now come down, one by one,' shouted up Sooty.

Go to **88**.

84

'Go back and have another look, Mary,' said Sooty. 'See who it is, then come and tell us.'

Mary sped off down the passage again. She had just put her hand on the doorknob to open the door when it was pushed back in her face. She jumped back in surprise. Standing in the doorway was her father.

'Where are you going, Mary?' he asked. Then, without waiting for a reply, he went on: 'Come with me. I want to talk to your brother and your friends.'

He strode down the passage in front of Mary and flung open the door of Sooty's bedroom. Of course, the room was empty, because everyone was next door in Mary's room.

'Where is everyone?' Mr Lenoir asked Mary, who was hovering anxiously behind him.

'In my room, Father,' she whispered.

Mr Lenoir opened the door of Sooty's room.

Go to **80**.

85

'What a place to hide smuggled goods,' said Dick. 'No one would ever find them here.'

'Come on,' said Sooty. 'Otherwise Timmy will never get his walk. There's a passage out of this pit that leads out on to the hillside. We'll have to do a bit of climbing when we get there. It's a steep path.'

'Are you sure you know the way out of here, Sooty?' asked Julian. 'We don't want to be lost down here for ever.'

'Of course I know the way,' said Sooty and, flashing his torch in front of him, he led them into a dark and narrow tunnel.

Go to **90**.

86

'Let's try Dick's idea,' said George. 'Can anyone think what we could use for a sling, though?'

'I know,' said Julian. 'A bath towel!'

'Yes, that might work,' agreed George.

'I'll go and get one from our bathroom,' said Sooty, and shot off. He reappeared a moment later carrying a big green towel. George took it from him and wrapped it around Timmy, holding the two short sides up above his back.

'Now, we need to tie some rope around the ends of the towel. Have you got a piece of rope, Sooty?' she asked.

Sooty found some rope and they gathered the towel-ends into a bunch, then tied the rope around them. George pulled the rope into a tight knot.

Go to **82**.

'Look out – here's Block!' said Sooty suddenly in a low voice. 'If Timmy comes around licking us or jumping up, pretend to try to drive him off as if he were a stray.'

They all behaved as if they hadn't seen Block, and gazed earnestly into the window of a shop. Timmy, who was feeling rather out of it, ran up to George and pawed at her, trying to make her notice him.

'Go away, dog!' said Sooty, flapping at the surprised Timmy. 'Go away! Stop following us about.'

Timmy thought this was some kind of game. He barked happily and ran around Sooty and George, giving them an occasional lick.

Then Block came up to them.

'Is that dog bothering you?' he asked in his flat, monotonous voice. 'Shall I throw a stone at him and make him go away?'

If you think Block throws a stone at the dog, go to **95**.
If you think he doesn't, go to **101**.

George climbed rapidly and easily down the ladder, and the others followed her. Soon they were all standing together at the bottom of the hole, in the enormous pit. It had a musty smell, and its walls were damp and greenish. Sooty swung his torch around, and the children could see passages leading off here and there.

'Where do they all lead to?' asked Julian in amazement.

'Well, I told you the hill was full of tunnels,' said Sooty. 'This pit is down in the hill, and these tunnels lead into the catacombs. No one explores them now, because so many people have been lost in them and never heard of again.'

'It's weird!' said Anne, and shivered.

Go to **85**.

89

Julian planted himself firmly with one foot on the path and one foot a short way down the hill. 'Right, George,' he said. 'Come on!'

George moved slowly and carefully off the path and down the hill, and caught hold of Julian's hand. Anne and Dick followed her, and finally Sooty inched his way gingerly down the hill, then stood up and took Dick's hand.

'Clasp each other's wrists,' called Julian. 'You'll get a better grip like that.'

They all did as Julian suggested, and Sooty was able to lean down and catch hold of Mary's hand. He pulled her to her feet, then helped her back up to the path. The others broke the chain and scrambled back to join Sooty and Mary.

'We'd better hurry now,' said Sooty, 'or we shan't have time to give Timmy a good run before we have to go back to the house for lunch.'

Go to **96**.

The tunnel ran slightly downwards and smelt rather nasty in places. Sometimes it opened into pits like the one under Mary's room. Sooty flashed his torch up into one of them.

'That one goes up into Mr Barling's house somewhere,' he said. 'Most of the old houses have openings into pits like ours.'

'There's daylight in front!' exclaimed Anne suddenly. 'Oh, good! I hate this tunnel.'

Sure enough, they soon came to a sort of shallow cave in the hillside. The children crowded into it and looked out. They were outside the hill, below the town, somewhere on the steep side of the cliff.

'Right,' said Sooty. 'Now, there are two paths up to the town wall from here.' He pointed to his left, where a narrow path ran steeply up some rocky steps and disappeared around a curve. 'That one is short, but very steep.' He swung around and pointed to his right. The others could see a wider path, which sloped up much more gently. 'That path is much less steep, but it's longer. Which way shall we go?'

If you think they should take the path to the left, go to **96**.
If you think they should go to the right, go to **102**.

91

The woman swung around to see where the stone

had come from, and saw the children and Block. She stormed over to them.

'What do you children mean by throwing stones at me?' she shouted.

'It wasn't one of us who threw a stone at you,' replied Julian politely, 'it was Block.' He pointed to Block, who was standing a few paces away.

'Rubbish!' said the angry woman. 'Why should he throw a stone at me? It must have been one of you children!'

At that moment they were joined by a young mother pushing a pram.

'It *was* that man who threw the stone,' she said to the furious woman. 'I saw him do it.'

The woman with the basket started to shout at Block, who simply gazed at her with his usual lack of expression.

'Why don't you answer me?' she shrieked. 'The least you can do is apologise!'

Go to **98**.

92

'It might be your father,' suggested Julian.

'I don't think so,' said Sooty. 'I thought I heard him snoring away in his bedroom. We could go and find out, though – see if he really is in there.'

'Well, for goodness' sake don't let's get caught,' said Julian, who didn't like the idea of prying about in his host's house.

They made their way back into the main part of

the house and stopped outside the door of Mr Lenoir's room. Julian paused, his hand on the door knob.

'Shall I open it?' he whispered.

If you think Julian should open it, go to **103**.
If you think he should leave it closed, go to **109**.

93

Over the next two or three days the children developed a routine. Timmy was taken out each morning for a long walk, and he soon got used to being hauled up and down in the laundry hamper. In the afternoons they either read or played games. They could have Timmy with them, because the buzzer always warned them if anyone was coming.

'It's quite a peaceful holiday,' said Julian. 'Nothing at all is happening.'

And then things *did* begin to happen, and once they had begun they never stopped!

Go to **100**.

94

Down the hill, Mary was dangling over the marsh, her scared white face turned up to the others.

'Look,' said Julian. 'If any of us tries to scramble down the hill to help her, we could easily end up in the marsh. I think the best thing to do would be to try to form a sort of human chain. I'll stand at the top and hold on to George's hand, then she can hold Anne's hand, then Dick, and last of all Sooty, who should be able to reach Mary.'

'Supposing one of us slips?' asked George.

'We shouldn't do,' replied Julian. 'We've all got rubber-soled shoes on, which should give us a good grip. Right, are you all ready?'

Go to **89**.

95

'Don't you dare!' said George at once. 'I don't mind the dog following us.'

'Block's deaf, silly,' said Sooty. 'It's no good talking to him.'

To George's horror Block picked up a big stone and threw it straight at Timmy! Fortunately Timmy jumped out of the way, and it missed him, but unluckily for Block the stone whistled past the legs of a woman who was walking up the street with a shopping-basket on her arm.

George grinned. Now Block would be in trouble!

Go to **91**.

96

If you've arrived from **89**, *score* ◁ ◁ ◁ ◁.

'I think we'd better try the steeper path,' said Dick. 'I'm longing to get into the town and see what it's like!'

'Oh, yes,' agreed George. 'Me too!'

They set off up the steep, rocky steps that curved around the side of the hill. Sooty had been right – the path, which went up very sharply, was more like a set of steps. Soon they reached the wall of the town. It was quite low, and they were all able to scramble over it easily. Timmy was pushed and pulled over by George and Julian, and they set off for a good walk.

The town was very old, and the shops were quaint, old-fashioned places with long, narrow windows and overhanging eaves. The children stopped to look in some of them.

Go to **87**.

97

Mr Barling said goodbye to the children and walked away. They were glad he had gone. None of them liked him very much.

'There's something odd about his eyes,' said Anne to herself with a little shudder.

The children soon forgot about Mr Barling and enjoyed the rest of their walk. George bought some meat for Timmy, making sure she went to a butcher that Sooty's mother didn't use, because she didn't want the butcher telling Mrs Lenoir that someone was buying dog meat!

They made their way back to the house the same way that they had come, down the hill to the cave, and back to the pit below the house. Timmy was packed into the laundry hamper again and hauled up into Mary's room. Sooty then took him back to the secret passage, leaving him with the meat that George had bought, and a bowl of fresh water.

Go to **93**.

98

'I'm afraid he's deaf,' said Sooty with a grin. 'He can't hear a word you're saying.'

Finding out that Block couldn't hear her only seemed to make the woman with the shopping-basket more annoyed, but eventually she stormed off, still muttering about people who threw stones at innocent passers-by.

Block looked at Timmy, who was still hovering around George's feet.

'I shall get rid of that dog,' he said flatly. 'I do not think you should encourage him to follow you. He might try to come home with you, and Mr Lenoir would not like that.'

He bent and picked up another stone.

Go to **101**.

99

Mary gave a shriek as she slid down the hill. Her hands scrabbled at the rough grass that covered the hill as she tried to get a grip and stop herself falling any further. She managed to catch hold of a small bush just before the bottom of the hill, and stopped with her feet just touching the edge of the marsh.

Sooty was about to start down the hill after his sister when Julian stopped him.

'Wait a minute, Sooty!' he said. 'We've got to decide the best way of doing this. If we go rushing down there we could all end up in the marsh. Now, let's think.'

Go to **94**.

100

One night Julian was woken by someone opening his door. He sat up at once.

'Who is it?' he asked.

'Me, Sooty,' said a voice, very quietly. 'I want you to come and see something.'

Julian woke Dick, and the two of them put on their dressing-gowns. Sooty led them across the landing to a funny little room tucked away in an odd wing of the house. It was a sort of box-room, full of trunks and boxes, old toys and general junk.

'Look,' said Sooty, taking them to the window. They saw that the little room had a view of the tower belonging to the house. The boys looked – and Julian gave an exclamation. Someone was signalling from the tower! A light flashed from it every now and again.

'Now, who's doing that?' said Sooty.

Go to **92**.

*If you've arrived from **98**, score* .

'Don't you dare!' said George immediately. 'I don't mind the dog following us.'

'Now, now,' said a voice nearby. 'What's all this about, Pierre? What's the trouble?'

They all turned and saw a tall man standing near them. He had narrow eyes, a long nose and a long chin.

'Oh, Mr Barling! I didn't see you,' said Sooty politely. 'Nothing's the matter, thank you. It's only that this dog is following us, and Block said he'd make it go away by throwing a stone at it. As George here is very fond of dogs, she got rather cross with him.'

'I see,' said Mr Barling. 'And who are your friends?'

'They've come to stay with us because their house has been damaged,' replied Sooty. He introduced the others to Mr Barling. 'They live at Kirrin,' added Sooty.

'Ah – at Kirrin!' said Mr Barling. 'Surely that is where that very clever scientist friend of your father's lives, Pierre?'

'Yes,' said George. 'He's my father.'

'I've heard of him – and of his experiments,' said Mr Barling. 'Mr Lenoir knows him well, I believe?'

'Not really,' said George, puzzled. 'They just write to one another, I think.'

Go to **97**.

102

'Let's go by the longer path,' said Anne. 'I've done enough climbing for a while, and we'll have to get back up into Mary's room later on!'

The others were all quite happy to take the wider path, so they set off with Timmy running ahead of them. He was very glad to be out in the fresh air again. He wasn't used to spending a lot of time indoors. It was quite a nice morning, with a slight breeze blowing, and there was no mist covering the marsh. The path was rather damp and slippery, though, because it had been covered by the mist for so long. All of them except Mary had on rubber-soled trainers, which gripped the path well, but

Mary's shoes had slippery leather soles, and she had trouble keeping her balance.

'Are you all right, Mary?' asked Anne, when Mary had stumbled for the third time. Just as Anne spoke, Mary slipped again, and this time she slid right off the path!

Go to **99**.

103

'I can't hear anything,' said Sooty. 'You'd better open it so that we can have a look.'

Very gingerly Julian pushed the door open and stuck his head round it. The room was very dark, even though there was a moon that night, because it had thick velvet curtains. As his eyes became accustomed to the dark, Julian could make out the large bed in the middle of the room.

'Is he in there?' whispered Dick.

If you think Mr Lenoir is in bed, go to **114**.
If you think he isn't, go to **120**.

104

If you've arrived from **118**, *score* ♋.

'Let's creep up to the tower,' said Sooty. 'We shall have to be jolly careful, though. The staircase up to it is very narrow, and there's nowhere much to hide if anyone suddenly comes out of the tower.'

'What's in the tower?' asked Dick as they made their way through the silent house.

'Nothing much,' said Sooty. 'Some chairs and a table, and a couple of bookcases. We only use it on hot summer days, because it gets plenty of breeze.'

They came to a little landing. From this a winding narrow staircase went up to the rounded tower. Moonlight fell on the stairs from a slit-like window.

'We'd better not all go up,' said Sooty. 'We should find it difficult to get down in a hurry. I'll go and see if I can spy anything through the keyhole.'

Go to **108**.

105

There was a creaking noise from the bed as Block sat up. Dick whisked himself behind the door. He heard Block get out of bed and walk out of the room, then up and down the passage. Dick stood stock still. He didn't dare try to get out of the room in case he bumped into Block. For a horrible moment he had a vision of being stuck behind Block's bedroom door until the morning, but he took a deep breath and tried to think sensibly.

Go to **107**.

106

Softly closing the door behind them, Sooty, Dick and Julian crept across the landing without speaking. It wasn't until they reached the passage to the back stairs that they stopped and caught their breath.

'Whew!' said Sooty. 'That was a *very* near thing! Come on, let's go and see if Block is in his room.'

They climbed the back stairs that led to the wing where Block and Sarah slept. Sooty pushed Block's door open very quietly. The room was on the opposite side of the house from his parents' bedroom, and it was full of moonlight. Sooty could see the humpy shape of Block's body under the bedclothes, and the black round patch that was his head.

He withdrew his head and pushed the other two boys back down the stairs.

Go to **112**.

107

After mulling things over, Dick decided that the best thing to do would be to wait in Block's room until he came back and got into bed again. Once Block was asleep, he could creep out and rejoin the others. He moved away from the door and ducked down beside a chest of drawers.

It seemed a very long time to poor Dick before he heard Block's footsteps coming back into the bedroom. He froze. Block got back into bed, and in a very short time his breathing became even, and Dick was able to slip out of the room.

'It's the strangest thing I've ever seen,' he said to himself as he made his way back to find the others.

'A man goes into a room and completely disappears! Where can he have gone?'

The other two were waiting at the bottom of the steps to the tower-room, and Dick told them of his strange experience.

'He simply vanished,' Dick said. 'Is there a secret passage leading out of Block's room, Sooty?'

'No,' replied Sooty. 'That part of the house is much newer than the rest of it. Who is that man, and what is he doing?'

'We simply *must* find out,' said Julian.

Go to **111**.

108

Sooty crept softly up the stairs. Julian and Dick waited at the bottom. There was a thick curtain over one of the windows there, and they got behind it, wrapping its folds around them for warmth.

Sooty crept up to the top. The tower-room had a stout oak door, studded and barred with iron. It was closed, so he bent down to see if he could see anything through the keyhole. He was annoyed to find that it had been blocked up with something. He pressed his ear to the door. He could hear a series of little clicks, but nothing else.

That's the click of the light they're using, thought Sooty. They're still at it. But why? Who to? Who is in the tower-room? I wish I knew!

Suddenly the clicking stopped. There was the

sound of someone walking across the floor of the tower, and then the rasp of the old-fashioned latch being pulled up. Sooty looked around frantically for somewhere to hide, but all he could see was a shallow niche on the other side of the stairs. Should he try to squeeze into that, or make a run for it down the stairs?

If you think he should hide in the niche, go to **116**.
If you think he should make a run for it, go to **121**.

109

If you've arrived from **114**, *score* ◁ ◁.

Suddenly the boys heard a loud, unmistakable snore, which gave them all the giggles!

'There's no doubt that's Father – sound asleep,' whispered Sooty. 'My mother certainly couldn't make a noise like that! Come on – let's go and see if Block is in his room.'

They crept across the landing and down the passage to the back stairs that led up to the wing where Block and Sarah slept. Sooty pushed Block's door open very quietly. The room was full of moonlight, and Sooty could see the humpy shape of Block's body under the bedclothes, and the black round patch that was his head.

He withdrew his head and pushed the other two boys back down the stairs.

Go to **112**.

If you've arrived from **113**, *score* ◯⊣ .

'I think we should follow him,' whispered Julian. 'Come on!'

Dick slipped out from behind the curtains, but Julian got his feet tangled in them and fell over. Sooty stayed to help him.

'Go on, Dick!' said Sooty. 'Don't wait for us!'

Dick ran down the passage in the direction the footsteps had taken. The moon came out again, and he could just catch an occasional glimpse of the signaller as he went through the patches of moonlight. Keeping well in the shadows himself, Dick darted after him. The man went along the passage that led to the staff bedrooms and, to Dick's enormous surprise, disappeared into Block's bedroom! Dick crept to the door, which had been left slightly open, and peeped in. There was no one in the room except Block, lying in bed. Dick edged closer, to try to see if it really was Block, but he bumped into a chair. The legs squeaked on the floor with a noise that sounded like a shriek in the silent house. Dick stood still, watching in horror as the figure on the bed rolled over and sighed. What on earth would he do if Block woke up and found him?

If you think Block wakes up, go to **105**.
If you think he stays asleep, go to **117**.

111

If you've arrived from **107**, *score* .

'Sooty,' asked Dick, 'when did you find out that someone was signalling from the tower?'

'It was some time ago,' replied Sooty. 'I couldn't sleep one night, so I went along to the little box-room to find an old book I'd seen in there. Suddenly I saw a light flashing from the tower. After that I went along there several more times, to see if I could see the signals again, and eventually I did. The first time I saw them there was a good moon, and the second time, too. So when I realised there was a good moon tonight I thought I'd creep along to the box-room to see if the signaller was at it again. And he was!'

Go to **122**.

112

If you've arrived from **119**, *score* .
If you've arrived from **106**, *score* .

'Was he there?' whispered Julian.

'Yes. So it can't be him signalling in the tower,' replied Sooty. 'Well, who can it be, then? Could there be a stranger in the house, living here in secret?'

'That's impossible,' said Julian, a little shiver running down his spine. 'Look – shall we go up to the tower and try to peep through the door? We might be able to see who it is.'

'Perhaps we should go back to the little box-room first,' suggested Dick, 'and see if the signalling is still going on. If it isn't, there'll be no point in going up to the tower-room.'

If you think they should go straight to the tower-room, go to **104**.

If you think they should go back to the box-room, go to **118**.

113

'Hold your nose!' hissed Julian.

Sooty grabbed his nose and pinched hard, and Julian seized a fold of the thick curtain and threw it around Sooty's head, muffling the small snorting noise he made as the sneeze escaped. To their great relief the footsteps went steadily on past.

Go to **110**.

114

Julian strained his eyes to see if there were one or two bodies in the bed. He thought he could see two shapes under the bedclothes, but the room was so dark it was very hard to be sure. Then one of the figures turned over, and at the same time muttered something which Julian couldn't catch, but he thought it had been a man's voice. The figure moved again, restlessly, and this time when it spoke the voice was definitely Mr Lenoir's.

'Who's there? Is somebody there?'

His heart thumping, Julian retreated, closing the door as quietly as he could. 'Quick!' he whispered to the others. 'Over here!'

The three boys crossed the landing and hid in the shadows of the passage on the other side.

'Perhaps he'll just turn over and go to sleep again,' whispered Sooty.

'Listen!' hissed Dick. They heard the bed give a loud creak. Perhaps Mr Lenoir was coming to look for them!

If you think Mr Lenoir goes back to sleep, go to **109**.
If you think he gets out of bed, go to **119**.

115

Their eyes were accustomed to the dark now, and they could see nearby a large chair in one corner of the room. Quickly the three of them crouched behind it, their hearts beating fast. They heard the bedroom door open and close, footsteps cross the floor, a creak as Mr Lenoir got back into bed, then silence.

It seemed to the three boys that they waited hours before the sound of breathing turned to rhythmic snores, but eventually they decided to risk leaving the room.

Go to **106**.

Sooty decided that there was no time to hurry down the stairs. All he could do was squeeze into the niche and hope that the person wouldn't see him or touch him as he went by. The moon went behind a cloud at that moment, and Sooty was thankful to know he was hidden in black shadow. The door of the tower-room opened and closed, and someone walked past the niche, actually brushing Sooty's arm as he went. Sooty jumped out of his skin, expecting to be hauled out of his hiding-place, but the person didn't seem to notice, and went on down the stairs. Sooty counted to a hundred, then slipped softly down the stairs to find the others.

Go to **110**.

Dick held his breath, but the figure on the bed rolled back again and settled down. Dick slid out of the room.

'That's the strangest thing I've ever seen,' he said to himself as he made his way back to join the others. 'A man goes into a room and completely disappears! Where can he have gone?'

The other two were waiting at the bottom of the steps to the tower-room, and Dick told them of his strange experience.

'He simply vanished,' Dick said. 'Are there any secret passages leading out of Block's room, Sooty?'

'No,' said Sooty. 'That part of the house is much newer than the rest of it. It's all very strange. Who is the man, and where does he come from, and what is he doing?'

'We really *must* find out,' said Julian. 'It's such a mystery!'

Go to **111**.

118

'I think Dick's right,' said Julian. 'If the signalling *has* stopped, then we can go back to our room and talk it over.'

They made their way back to the little box-room and looked out of the window at the tower. For a moment or two nothing happened, then the flashing started again, in the same pattern that they had seen before – a flash, a pause, another flash, then a longer pause. Julian knew Morse Code quite well, and he was reasonably certain that the person doing the signalling wasn't using that. It was all very strange.

Go to **104**.

119

There was silence for a few moments, then they heard the *pad*, *pad*, *pad* of footsteps coming towards the door. The three boys pressed themselves back into the shadows.

Mr Lenoir opened the bedroom door and peered out, then he seemed to shrug his shoulders, as if deciding he had been mistaken. He came out of the room and padded off along the landing.

'He's probably going to the bathroom,' whispered Sooty when his father was out of earshot. 'Come on, we'll go and see if Block is in his room!'

They climbed the back stairs that led to the wing where Block and Sarah slept. Sooty pushed Block's door open very quietly. The room was on the opposite side of the house from his parents' bedroom, and it was full of moonlight. Sooty could see the humpy shape of Block's body under the bedclothes, and the black round patch that was his head.

He withdrew his head and pushed the other two boys back down the stairs.

Go to **112**.

120

Julian strained his eyes to see if there were one or two bodies in the bed. The room was very dark, and it was hard to be sure, so he opened the door a bit wider and tiptoed into the room, followed by Dick and Sooty. Then suddenly they all froze. Somewhere in the house, not very far away, a door had been closed, and they could hear heavy footsteps coming towards them.

'My father!' hissed Sooty. 'He's coming back from the bathroom. What shall we do? He's bound to catch us!'

'We'll have to hide in here,' whispered Julian.
'Quick – close the door!'

Go to **115**.

121

Sooty knew that the tower door was very heavy and
liable to stick, so he thought he had just got time to
make a dash for it down the stairs. He guessed that
Julian and Dick might have hidden behind the
curtain, so he scrambled behind it, falling over
Dick's feet as he went. He was just in time. They
could hear the door open and close, and then the
sound of footsteps coming down the stairs. A certain
amount of light was coming through the window,
and Julian could see both Dick and Sooty very
clearly. As he watched, Sooty started to make
agonised gestures. He was going to sneeze!

Go to **113**.

122

'Where does that window in the tower look out –
towards the sea, or inland?' asked Julian.

'Seaward,' said Sooty at once. 'There's something or someone out at sea who receives those
signals. Let's go up to the tower and have a look,
shall we?'

They went back to the tower-room and stood

looking out of the window. It was dark, for the moon was behind a cloud, but when it came out they could see the flat marsh stretching away to the sea. There was no mist that night.

'Suddenly Julian clutched Dick's arm.

'Look!' he said in excitement. 'There's a light on the marsh – see?'

'It's moving!' said Sooty, straining his eyes to see. 'Or is that just my imagination?'

If you think the light is moving, go to **127**.
If you think it is stationary, go to **133**.

123

They were discussing the events of the night before at breakfast. Block came in to see if they had finished, but Anne didn't notice him.

'What does Mr Barling smuggle?' she began. Immediately she got a hard kick on the ankle from Sooty, who was sitting opposite her. She stared at him in pain and surprise. 'Why did you . . . ?' she began, and got another kick. Then she saw Block. 'He's deaf,' she protested. 'He can't hear anything.'

Sooty waited until Block had gone out of the room with a pile of dirty plates. Then he smiled at Anne. 'I'm sorry I had to kick you,' he apologised, 'but I'm not sure that Block doesn't understand what we say.'

'Nonsense,' said Anne crossly, still rubbing her bruised ankle.

'Well, let's try an experiment,' suggested George.

'One of us could drop a plate behind him. If he turns around, we'll know that he heard the noise. If he doesn't, we can be sure he's deaf.'

'That's a good idea,' said Dick. 'Won't we get into trouble if we break a plate, though?'

Sooty picked up his cereal bowl and handed it to Dick.

'Use that,' he said. 'It's got a nasty crack in it anyway.'

When Block reappeared with a plate of scrambled eggs, Dick waited until he had put it on the sideboard and begun to spoon it on to plates. Then Dick picked up the bowl and threw it down on to the stone floor. The bowl shattered into dozens of pieces. The six children sat with their eyes fixed on Block's back.

If you think Block turns around, go to **129**.
If you think he doesn't move, go to **134**.

124

When they got back to Mary's room that morning, they pulled Timmy up from the pit and let him out of the basket. 'We'll put him in the secret passage as usual,' said George, 'and I'll put some biscuits in with him. I got some nice ones for him this morning.'

She went to the door – but just as she was about to unlock it and take the dog to Sooty's room, Timmy gave a small growl. George took her hand away from the door at once and looked down at Timmy.

He was standing stiffly, the hackles on his neck up, his eyes fixed on the door. George put her finger to her lips warningly.

Go to **128**.

125

'You see!' said Sooty. 'He *isn't* deaf after all! I always suspected he heard more than people realised.'

'I'm sorry to disappoint you,' said Julian, 'but we still can't be sure if he's deaf or not. Look at the floor. Some of the bits of china from the broken bowl have landed right by the sideboard. Block might have seen them and guessed what had happened.'

Sooty frowned. 'Well, I think we'd be wise to watch what we say in front of him, even so,' he said.

Go to **131**.

126

Timmy turned and looked at George, his tail wagging.

'It's all right,' she said to the others. 'There's no one there now. Timmy always knows. We'd better get him back into your room quickly, Sooty, while the coast is clear. Who could it have been, do you think, snooping outside?'

'Probably Block,' answered Sooty. He unlocked the door and peered out. There was no one in the passage, and he waved to George to tell her that it was all right to take Timmy into his room.

Soon Timmy was safely in the secret passage, crunching biscuits, and the others went to wash their hands for lunch.

Go to **132**.

127

If you've arrived from **133**, *score* ⌒ .

The tiny pinpoint of light seemed to be bobbing up and down, and, as the boys watched, more tiny dots of light appeared behind it. Then the moon came out, flooding everywhere with silvery light, and the

boys could see nothing but the moonshine. They waited for a while, and then the moon went behind a cloud again. The row of tiny lights could still be seen, and this time the watching boys could clearly see that the lights were moving.

'Smugglers!' whispered Sooty. 'Smugglers – coming over a secret path from the sea to Castaway Hill!'

Go to **130**.

128

'Someone's outside,' whispered George. 'Timmy smelt them. You all talk very loudly, and I'll put Timmy into the cupboard.'

The others quickly began to play Snap, shouting and laughing. George bundled Timmy into the cupboard, then stared at the door handle. It was turning very slowly! Someone meant to open the door without being heard, and come in unexpectedly. As George watched, the person outside realised that the door was locked, and the handle turned back the other way. George wondered if they were still there. She didn't want to open the door, but she knew that Timmy would know if there was anyone there. She let him out of the cupboard and pointed towards the door. He ran up to it and sniffed hard.

Go to **126**.

Block swung around from the sideboard and looked at the children.

'Which one of you dropped that bowl?' he asked. Sooty's mouth dropped open in astonishment. For months Block had been pretending that he was deaf, and now all of a sudden he seemed to be admitting that he could hear after all!

'Er – it was me, Block,' he said. 'Shall I get a dustpan and brush to sweep up the pieces?'

'I shall get them,' said Block, and left the room.

Go to **125**.

130

The three girls were very excited the next day when the boys told them about their adventure of the night before.

'I do wish you'd come and told me and Anne,' said George.

'There wasn't time,' said Julian. He thought for a moment. 'I think that the smugglers probably came over from France, anchored as near to the marsh as they could, waited for a signal to tell them that the coast was clear – probably the signal from the tower – then they came across the marsh. No doubt there was someone waiting to receive the goods they brought – someone at the edge of the marsh, below the hill.'

'But who?' asked Dick. 'Everyone says Mr Barling is a smuggler, but it can't have been him, because the signal came from this house.'

Go to **123**.

131

If you've arrived from **125**, *score* $\bigcirc$.

After breakfast they took Timmy out, using the laundry hamper as usual. It was amazing how quickly he had got used to being hauled up and down, and he jumped happily into the hamper as soon as he saw it.

That morning they again met Block, who stared with great interest at Timmy. He plainly recognised him as the dog he had seen before.

'We'll pretend he's a stray who always meets us,' said Julian in a low voice, so they let Timmy run around them as they walked. Block came up to them.

'That dog seems to be a friend of yours,' he said in his flat voice.

'Oh, yes,' replied Julian. 'I think he's adopted us. He joins us every morning for a walk.'

Block gave Julian a strange look, then walked on, glancing back at the children from time to time as he went.

Go to **124**.

They were all starving and were glad when lunch was served. Block gave them some soup, then left the room. Suddenly, to the children's intense surprise and fright, they heard Timmy barking loudly!

'Listen to Timmy!' said Julian. 'He must be somewhere near here, in that passage. His bark sounds weird from a distance, but anyone who heard it would know that it was a dog barking.'

'It's the bark he gives when he's excited,' said George. 'I expect he's chasing a rat. Oh dear, there he goes again. I hope he catches the rat soon and settles down.'

Block came back at that moment. There was no sound from Timmy for some minutes, and then, just as the children had begun to think that he must have caught his rat, he barked again.

Go to **135**.

133

The moon had come out from behind the clouds again, and the marsh looked eerie in the silvery light. Dick gave a sudden shiver. There was something very strange and haunting about the marsh, something that made Dick think of all the people who had been lost on it.

Julian was staring intently at the light. 'It's not

moving,' he said finally. 'It did look as though it was, but now I'm sure it's stationary. I wonder what it is? It's a very white light, not like the light from a torch or a car's headlights.'

'It's probably the light of the moon reflected in one of the pools of water on the marsh,' said Sooty. 'I've noticed that before – thought there was a light out there, I mean.'

Dick suddenly gave a gasp, which made the others jump.

'Look!' he said, pointing out at the marsh. 'Away over there – isn't that another light?'

Go to **127**.

134

Much to their disappointment, Block continued to dish out scrambled eggs in his usual mechanical fashion. He saw the broken bowl when he turned around to bring the plates to the table.

'What happened to that bowl?' he asked.

'Oh, it slipped out of my hand,' said Sooty airily. 'It was badly cracked, anyway.'

Block finished serving breakfast, then went to get a broom to sweep up the bits of china.

'It looks as though he really *is* deaf,' said Anne.

'Maybe he is,' replied Sooty, 'but I don't think we can trust him. He can probably lip-read, you know. A great many deaf people can.'

Go to **131**.

Julian watched Block very closely. He went on serving the meat but looked around at the children intently, as if he wanted to watch each child's expression, or see if they said anything.

'That was jolly good soup,' said Julian to the others. 'I must say Sarah's a marvellous cook.'

'*Woof! Woof!*' came Timmy's voice from far away behind the walls.

'George, I think your mother makes the best fruit cake I ever tasted,' said Dick rather desperately. 'I wonder how they're getting on with the repairs to Kirrin Cottage?'

'*Woof!*' said Timmy again.

Go to **138**.

Go to **138**.

136

'You can't go home,' said Sooty. 'If one of you goes, I'm sure my stepfather would say that all of you have to go, and we'd never discover what's going on here.'

George sat silently for a while. Then she gave a sigh and got up.

'Well, I suppose I shall have to stay here with you, but I'm going to telephone my parents anyway. I'd like to know what's happening at home.'

She went downstairs to the hall where the telephone stood on a table, and dialled her parents' number. There was a long wait, and then she heard the *brr – brr, brr – brr* of the telephone at Kirrin Cottage.

If you think someone answers the phone, go to **142**.
If you think no one answers, go to **148**.

137

George's hand closed round Timmy's leather collar, and she hung on tight. Block's legs were flailing about, and Sooty, Julian and Dick were all struggling with the heavy curtains, trying to wrap them around him. There were muffled yells of rage from the struggling figure, and Timmy was getting more and more excited, growling in a menacing way and baring his teeth. George put both hands on his collar to try to hang on to him. She was terrified that any moment he would bark, which would bring everyone else in the house to see what was going on.

'Sh, sh, Timmy, please,' whispered George. 'Don't you dare bark!'

Suddenly Timmy gave a really sharp tug and pulled George forwards. She tripped and fell, letting go of Timmy's collar.

Go to **152**.

138

Block served everyone and then disappeared.

'I hope Block *is* as deaf as a post,' said Julian. 'I

could have sworn I saw a surprised look in his eyes when Timmy barked.'

'Well, if he could hear him, which I don't believe,' said George, 'he must have been jolly surprised to see us talking away and not paying any attention to it!'

The others were still laughing at this when the door opened and Mr Lenoir walked in.

'I just came to see if you were all enjoying yourselves, and that Block is looking after you properly,' said Mr Lenoir, smiling at them all. He irritated the children because he always spoke to them as if they were very small.

At that moment Timmy barked again! Mr Lenoir looked startled, and stared at the children. They made no sign of having heard anything. Julian felt certain that Mr Lenoir had been told that a dog had been heard in the children's room, and he had come to investigate. They were all desperately hoping that Mr Lenoir would leave the room before Timmy barked again.

If you think that Timmy barks again before Mr Lenoir goes, go to **144**.
If you think he doesn't, go to **150**.

139

'Come and tell me when I can let Timmy out,' whispered George to Sooty as they went upstairs. Sooty nodded, and as soon as he reached his own room he had a good look around. There was no sign of Block in any of the rooms that the children used, so he went to tell George that the coast was clear. As he came out of the door at the end of the passage and walked across the landing, he noticed two black shoes sticking out under the thick velvet curtains drawn across the landing window. Sooty grinned. He was sure he knew who those feet belonged to!

'Block's spying on us,' said Sooty to himself. 'I've got an idea!'

He ran along to join the others.

'Listen,' he said. 'Block's hiding behind the landing curtains, and I know he's trying to spy on us to see if we really have got a dog here. Let's all go on to the landing, and I'll shout out that I can see a burglar. I'll pounce on Block and knock him over, and Dick and Julian can pull the curtains down on top of him!'

'While you're doing that, I'll slip by with Timmy,' said George. 'I just hope Timmy doesn't give Block a good nip as we go past!'

Go to **143**.

140

The boys unwound the bundle of curtains, and Block got to his feet, crimson with rage and fright.

'I won't stand for this!' he raged. 'Look at my leg, sir! I've been bitten! Only a dog could do that!' He started to pull up his trouser leg, and the children looked at each other in horror. Once Mr Lenoir saw the bite he would know that there was a dog somewhere in the house. Then suddenly the front door bell rang!

'You'd better go down and answer that, Block,' said Mr Lenoir. 'I'm expecting a visitor – show him into my study, please.'

'Very good, sir,' replied Block, and he went downstairs, straightening his rumpled jacket and smoothing his hair with his hands as he went. George felt almost sick with relief as she watched him walk away.

Mr Lenoir turned back to the children. 'Get to bed, all of you!' he said angrily. 'How dare you behave like that! If Block leaves, it will be all your fault!' He stormed downstairs, followed by Mrs Lenoir.

'Goodness,' said Dick as he got into bed, 'wouldn't it be wonderful if Block did leave! I do hope he does. Perhaps he won't be here tomorrow!'

If you think Block is there in the morning, go to **149**.
If you think he isn't, go to **156**.

141

Block came in with the pudding at that moment, his face as blank as ever.

'Funny how Mr Lenoir thought there was a dog barking!' said Julian, and the others backed him up valiantly. If Block could read their lips he wouldn't be able to tell whether there *had* been a dog barking or not.

The children escaped to Sooty's room afterwards

and discussed what they were going to do about Timmy.

'Does your stepfather know the secret way behind the walls of Smuggler's Top?' George asked Sooty.

'He might,' said Sooty. 'I think he probably knows that there are secret passages, but I'm not sure if he knows where the entrances are.'

'I can't risk him finding Timmy,' said George. 'I'm going home.'

Go to **136**.

142

The telephone rang for a very long time, and George was just about to put the receiver down when a voice at the other end said, 'Hello.'

'Is that you, Father?' said George. 'It's me, George.'

'Oh, hello, what can I do for you?' said the voice at the other end.

'Well, I was wondering how things were at Kirrin Cottage,' replied George.

'We're getting on all right,' said the voice, 'but them rooms upstairs won't be ready for a long time. Anyway, why do you need to ring me up to ask me that, son?'

George was rather surprised. Even though her father knew she wished she was a boy, he certainly never called her son!

'I just wondered how you and Mother were,' she said uncertainly.

'Why are you ringing me to ask me 'ow your mother is?' came the reply. 'Isn't she there in the 'ouse with you?'

George felt completely baffled, as if she were having a peculiar dream. Then suddenly she realised what had happened.

Go to **145**.

143

The children went out to the landing. They could see the curtain twitch slightly as Block tried to see them through the gap in the middle. Then Sooty gave a blood-curdling yell and flung himself on Block, shouting at the top of his voice.

'A burglar! Help, there's a burglar here!'

Block began to struggle, and Sooty gave him a couple of sharp punches. Julian and Dick tugged violently at the curtains, which fell on Block's head. The heavy curtain pole came down too, knocking him sideways.

George started to hurry across the landing with Timmy, who dug his heels in and tried hard to see the fun. George had terrible trouble hanging on to him. All at once, Timmy twisted away from her and leapt towards Block. George made a grab at his collar.

If you think she catches him, go to **137**.
If you think she misses, go to **152**.

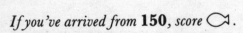

144

If you've arrived from **150**, *score* ⊂⊐.

Timmy gave another loud bark, and the children's hearts sank.

'Did you hear that noise?' asked Mr Lenoir.

'Er – what noise, Mr Lenoir?' asked Julian.

Timmy barked again.

'Don't be foolish!' snapped Mr Lenoir. 'There's the noise again!' At that moment a gull called outside the window, circling in the breeze.

'Oh – that gull? Yes, we often hear the gulls,' said Dick brightly.

Timmy barked yet again. Mr Lenoir looked at the

children. He was in a very bad temper indeed by now.

'Can't you hear that? Tell me what *that* noise is!' he said.

The children all pretended to listen very carefully. 'I can't hear anything,' said Dick, 'except the wind and the seagulls.'

'I tell you, it's a dog!' said Mr Lenoir. 'And you all know it. Now just you listen to me. That *is* a dog, and when I catch him I'll send him to the strays' home, and I'll see to it that the owner never gets him back. Do you understand?'

Without waiting for an answer, he stormed out of the room.

Go to **141**.

145

George chuckled. Obviously it wasn't her father who had answered the phone, but one of the workmen. He must have a son called George, and thought that was who she was!

'Look, you've made a mistake,' she said into the receiver. 'I'm not your son, George. I'm the daughter of the people who own Kirrin Cottage. Are my parents there?'

'No, they've gone away,' replied the man. 'The noise was too much for your father, so they decided to go away for a week or two until things were better.'

'Do you know where they went?' asked George.

'Afraid not, love,' he replied. 'They just said they'd give us a ring before they came back.'

'All right. Thank you,' said George. 'Goodbye.'

She put the receiver down and turned to go back upstairs to the others. At that moment Mrs Lenoir came out of the drawing-room.

'Ah, George,' she said. 'I was just coming to find you. I had a phone call from your parents this morning – they've had to leave the cottage because of the noise.'

'I know,' said George miserably. 'I was just ringing them, and I spoke to one of the workmen.'

Go to **151**.

146

The next evening Mr Lenoir was out, and the children spent the hour before bedtime in the drawing-room with Mrs Lenoir, playing Monopoly. They were half way through the game when the telephone rang.

Mrs Lenoir went out to the hall to answer it. After a few minutes she came back.

'That was your father, George,' she said. 'He's coming here tomorrow, but your mother has decided to stay on at her cousin's for a while. Your father is very interested in my husband's work – they're working on the same sort of experiments, you know.'

They were all a little disappointed that Aunt Fanny wouldn't be coming, because she was much easier to get on with than Uncle Quentin, but there was nothing they could do about it. They finished their game, said good night to Mrs Lenoir and went up to bed.

Go to **139**.

147

George left Timmy and ran back to join the others. Block was still yelling and struggling, with the curtains wrapped around him like a cocoon. Suddenly Mr Lenoir appeared in the hall below, with Mrs Lenoir beside him.

'What's all this?' he thundered. 'Have you gone mad? What on *earth* are you all doing?'

'We've caught a burglar and tied him up,' panted Sooty.

Mr Lenoir came up the stairs. He saw the kicking figure wrapped in the curtains and looked at the children in amazement. 'A burglar! Where did you find him?'

'He was hiding behind the curtains,' said Julian. 'We managed to get hold of him and tie him up before he could escape.'

From the bundle of curtains came the muffled sound of a voice yelling, 'Let me go! I've been bitten! Let me go!'

'Good heavens!' said Mr Lenoir. 'You've got Block in there! Let him go immediately.'

'But Father – it can't be Block,' protested Sooty. 'Why would Block be hiding behind the curtains?'

Go to **140**.

148

George let the telephone ring for a long time, but there was no reply. She put the receiver down and turned to go back upstairs to the others. She had to blink tears out of her eyes as she went, because she was missing her home and her parents, and she was constantly worried about Timmy.

Just then Mrs Lenoir came out of the drawing-room.

'Ah, George, my dear,' she said. 'I was just coming to look for you. I had a telephone call from your parents this morning. The noise that the builders were making was too much for your father, and he and your mother have gone away for a week or two to stay with her cousin.'

Go to **151**.

149

If you've arrived from **159**, *score* ◁▷ ◁▷.

After they had finished breakfast, Block came into the playroom to collect the plates. His face was as expressionless as usual, but his eyes gleamed in a nasty way as he looked at Sooty.

'You look out for yourself, Pierre,' he said in a soft, menacing voice. 'I know you've got a dog somewhere. You can't deceive *me*. You'd better watch your step!'

Sooty made no reply, but he bared his teeth and growled in a way that made the others laugh, except George. She felt that there was something truly evil about the manservant, and she gave a little shiver.

Go to **153**.

150

Mr Lenoir lingered for a few minutes, asking the children questions about what they had been doing, and whether they had seen this or that sight in the town. Finally he went to the door, then turned back to look at them.

'Go on with your lunch,' he said. 'I am pleased you are all enjoying yourselves here.'

The door was just closing behind him when Timmy gave the most enormous bark, very close at hand.

The door flew open again and Mr Lenoir came back in to the room. He glared at the children.

Go to **144**.

151

If you've arrived from **145**, *score* ◯.

'My husband has written to them asking if they

would like to come and stay here,' went on Mrs Lenoir. 'I expect one of them will ring when they get the letter, to tell us if they'd like to come or not.'

'Oh, I see,' said George. 'Thank you very much, Mrs Lenoir.'

George trudged back upstairs to the others and told them what had happened.

'So whatever happens, Timmy and I can't go home,' she finished sadly.

'Never mind, old thing,' said Sooty. 'We love having you all here, don't we, Mary?'

Mary nodded. She never said very much.

'The thing that worries me most is that if my parents come here, they're bound to ask me where Timmy is, and what on earth shall I tell them?' said George.

'Say he's staying with someone who lives in the town,' suggested Sooty.

George's face brightened. 'That's a good idea,' she said.

Go to **146**.

152

If you've arrived from **137**, *score* ◯⊲.

Timmy could see one of Block's legs sticking out, and he pounced on it and gave it a sharp nip! There was an agonised yell from Block, who kicked out wildly. Timmy worried at the waving leg for a few seconds, then George gave him a sharp smack. Shocked, Timmy let go of the leg and followed George along to her bedroom. George had never hit him before, and Timmy was very worried. He crept under the bed and gazed up at her with sad brown eyes full of dismay.

'Oh, Timmy, I'm sorry,' said George, getting down on her knees and giving him a hug. 'I *had* to smack you, to make you stop.'

Go to **147**.

153

George had a terrible shock later that morning. Sooty came to find her, looking agitated. 'I say, George!' he said. 'What do you think? Your father's going to have *my* room. I've got to share Julian's and Dick's room. Sarah is taking all my things from my room to theirs this very minute. I hope we shall have a chance to get Timmy out all right, before your father comes!'

'Oh, Sooty!' exclaimed George in despair. 'I'd better go and see if I can get Timmy out straight away.'

George went along to Sooty's room. The door was wide open and Block was inside, cleaning busily. And there he stayed, all morning.

Go to **157**.

George had been in and out of the secret passage so often in the past few days that she was able to open and close the entrance with no trouble. She had taken to keeping a small torch in her pocket all the time in case she suddenly had to use the passage, and now she pulled it out of her pocket and turned it on. Together she and Timmy walked down the stone steps and along the narrow way until they came to a dead end. She knew that the study entrance was on her right, and she felt around until she touched the knob that made one of the oak panels in the wall slide back. Sooty had told her where it was the first time they had come through the passage.

With her hand on the knob, George paused. Supposing Mr Lenoir was in his study. It would be dreadful to open the panel and come face to face with him.

Then she heard a door opening, and two voices. It sounded as though Mr Lenoir *was* there, and Block had come in to speak to him. A few moments later the door was closed. But had Mr Lenoir left the room with Block, or was he still in there? Taking a deep breath, George pressed the knob.

If you think Mr Lenoir has left the room, go to **160**.
If you think he is still in there, go to **165**.

George made up her mind that she was going to get Timmy out of the passage as soon as possible, so she slipped downstairs and tried the door of the study, but it was locked. Then she went out of the side door and into the yard. The window of the study looked out on the yard, and George thought she might be able to get in that way. She tried the window, but it was firmly closed. She went back into the hall. Suddenly she heard Mr Lenoir's voice. In a panic, George lifted the lid of a big chest nearby and climbed hurriedly into it. She closed the lid over herself and crouched there, her heart beating fast. She heard Mr Lenoir cross the hall and unlock the study door. The door opened and closed, but George didn't hear the key turn again. That meant the door was unlocked!

Go to **164**.

The following morning the children went along to the playroom for breakfast, only to find that the room was empty. The table had been laid, and the cereals and toast were on the sideboard, but there was no sign of Block, who was usually in and out of the room with bacon and eggs.

'I wonder if he *has* left,' said Anne. 'Wouldn't it be marvellous not to have him snooping about?'

'It would be too good to be true if he really has gone,' said Sooty. 'I've got a feeling that it suits Block very well to work here.'

'What do you mean?' asked George.

'It's just a feeling,' replied Sooty. 'I can't prove it, but I'm sure Block is up to no good, and whatever he's doing, this house is involved!'

Go to **159**.

157

George got more and more worried about Timmy. He would miss his walk, and he would need some food and water before very long. She hovered around Sooty's room for ages, getting in the way of Sarah as she moved Sooty's things to the room he would share with Julian and Dick.

Block gave George some rather curious looks as she kept popping out of the playroom and into Sooty's room, each time with a less convincing excuse. Finally Block left the room, and George darted in, but he returned almost at once and she had to leave. Again Block left and went down the passage, and again the desperate George rushed into Sooty's room. Block was back before she could get to Timmy.

'What are you doing in here?' he asked. 'Just go away. This room has to be kept clean for your father.'

George went – and once more waited for Block to go. It was nearly lunchtime, and he would have to go downstairs soon. Sure enough, a minute or two later she saw him go along the passage towards the door. But as she rushed next door to Sooty's room he turned around and saw her.

'Please get ready for lunch now,' he told her.

Blow! thought George. No chance of getting Timmy out now. Block would be sure to get her into trouble if she missed lunch.

As soon as the meal was over, she left the play-room and hurried to Sooty's room, but as she put her hand on the door handle, George had a dreadful thought. Supposing Block had locked the door?

If you think the door is locked, go to **162**.
If you think it isn't, go to **169**.

158

George decided that she would try to find the dining-room entrance, so she walked back along the passage, holding her torch in front of her, until she came to the part of the passage that Sooty had said went past the dining-room. She started to feel all around the walls for something to make the panel slide back – a knob, or a lever, but she couldn't find anything. In the end she gave up. George realised that, even if she found the device that opened the panel, she ran the risk of bumping into Block or Sarah clearing the table after lunch. There was nothing for it but to go back. She retraced her steps down the passage and settled down to decide the best thing to do.

Go to **171**.

159

They all sat down and started breakfast. Sarah came in while they were eating their cereal.

'Where's Block, Sarah?' asked Sooty.

'He's gone down to the doctor,' answered Sarah. 'He said he'd got a bad leg which he wanted the doctor to look at, so he went off to morning surgery. He should be back quite soon.'

'Oh, well,' said George after Sarah had left the room. 'Block leaving was too good to be true!'

They all discussed what they were going to do that morning.

'Well, the first thing to do is to get Timmy out of the passage,' said George. 'We'll have to keep an eye out for Block, though.'

Go to **149**.

160

If you've arrived from **171**, *score* ⌒⌒.

The panel slid back, and George looked cautiously into the study. It was empty! She tiptoed over to the door and tried the handle. It turned easily. She looked at Timmy, who was waiting in the entrance to the passage.

'I'm going to shut you in again for a moment, Timmy,' she said in a low voice. 'I'm going to check that the coast is clear, then I'll be back to let you out if all's well.'

She felt around for the place on the panelling to close the entrance. It was difficult to find, and George had to force herself to keep calm as she searched. She was so frightened that Mr Lenoir would come in and find her. Eventually she found the right spot, the panel swung smoothly into place, and she darted out of the study and into the hall. Just as she was looking around to see if there was anyone there, she heard the sound of Mr Lenoir's voice in the room across the hall. In a panic George lifted the lid of a big chest nearby and climbed hurriedly into it. She closed the lid over herself and crouched there, her heart beating fast. She heard Mr Lenoir cross the hall and open the study door. The door closed, but George didn't hear the key turn. That meant the door was unlocked!

Go to **164**.

161

If you've arrived from **173**, *score* ◁.

Mr Lenoir stirred, opened his eyes and sat up. He looked at George in amazement, which swiftly turned to rage.

'And what exactly do you think you're doing? How dare you come into my study and mess about like this?'

George was frightened. She ran to the door, but Mr Lenoir caught her before she could open it.

'What are you doing in my study? Do you think it's funny to play tricks on me? I'll soon teach you that it isn't!'

He opened the door and called for Block, who appeared from the dining-room, his face as blank as usual. Mr Lenoir wrote something on a piece of paper and handed it to him. Block read it and nodded.

Go to **167**.

162

The handle turned, but the door was locked. George was in despair. She went to find Sooty.

'Sooty!' she said. 'Block has locked the door of your room and I can't get in to let Timmy out. I'll have to use the entrace in your stepfather's study.'

'You can't,' said Sooty, looking alarmed. 'He's using it – he's got the records of all his experiments in there, ready to show to your father.'

'I don't care!' said George desperately. 'I've *got* to get into that passage, or Timmy may starve!'

'There are quite a lot of mice and rats he could kill and eat,' said Sooty consolingly.

'Yes, but there's no fresh water,' replied George, 'and he needs that all the time.'

Sooty gave her shoulder a pat. 'Cheer up, old thing,' he said. 'We'll find a way of getting Timmy out, you wait and see.'

Go to **155**.

163

Julian, Dick and the others rushed out at once, just in time to see Block shove George roughly into her room and lock the door.

'What are you doing?' Julian asked indignantly.

'Mr Lenoir gave me orders to punish that girl,' replied Block, giving Julian a push. 'Now go back to your own room and leave her alone!' He went off along the passage.

Julian called through the door to George: 'George! Whatever's happened?'

Through the locked door, George told him. All the others came and listened too.

'I don't care about being punished,' finished George, 'but I'm worried about Timmy.'

'I don't think there's much we can do,' answered Julian, 'except wait until you're let out tomorrow. Nobody seems to have thought about poor Anne – all her things are in there with you. Where is she going to sleep?'

'She can sleep in my room,' said Mary. 'I can lend her a nightdress.'

Go to **172**.

If you've arrived from **160**, *score* ⌒⌒ .

George knelt in the dark chest and considered matters. She had to get into the study and open the passage to reach Timmy. What she would do with him then she wasn't sure. Perhaps Sooty would know of someone in the town who could take care of him.

She could hear the sound of Mr Lenoir coughing, and the shuffling of papers. Suddenly he gave an exclamation of annoyance. He said something in an irritable voice, which sounded like, 'Now where did I put that?' Then the study door opened suddenly

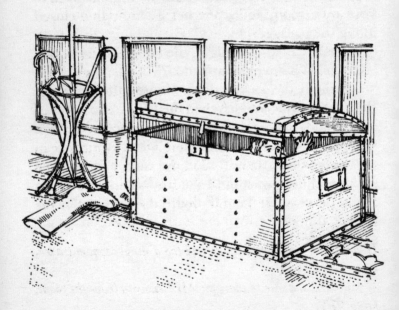

and he came out. George, who had lifted the lid a little to get some fresh air, let it go too quickly. As Mr Lenoir passed the chest, the lid fell into place with a slight bang. George froze. Had he heard it?

If you think Mr Lenoir heard the bang, go to **170**.
If you think he didn't, go to **176**.

165

The panel slid silently back, and George peeped into the study. On the other side of the room she could see the big desk, and seated in a chair in front of it was Mr Lenoir! Fortunately he had his back to George, so she quickly pressed the knob that closed the panel and stood in the dark, shaking a little with fright at her close shave. Timmy sat patiently beside her. George tried frantically to remember what Sooty had told her about the passage. She shut her eyes and tried to recall their first journey along it, just after they had arrived at Smuggler's Top. Surely Sooty had said that there was an entrance in the dining-room as well as in the study? Should she try to find that, or should she stay where she was in the hope that Mr Lenoir would soon go out of the study?

If you think she should try to find the dining-room entrance, go to **158**.
If you think she should wait for Mr Lenoir to leave the room, go to **171**.

George sat down on the bed and stared at the floor in dismay. She was locked in! She took a deep breath and tried to think sensibly. Surely the others would miss her before long, and come and see what had happened? But what if Block had taken the key out of the door? It would be very difficult for them to explain what George was doing in Sooty's room, when none of his things were left in it. Then George remembered that, when they had all arrived at Smuggler's Top, Sooty had taken them into the secret passage through an entrance in his step-father's study. If they could get *in* that way, then she could get *out*.

She jumped off the bed and opened the cupboard door again.

'Come on, Timmy!' she said quietly. 'Back into the passage!'

Timmy was heartily sick of the passage, but he followed George obediently.

Go to **154**.

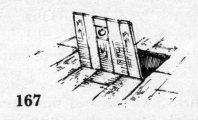

167

'I've told Block to take you to your room and lock you in,' said Mr Lenoir angrily. 'You are to have nothing but bread and water for the rest of the day.

Perhaps that will teach you to behave yourself in future.'

'My father won't be very pleased that you're punishing me like this,' said George in a shaky voice.

'I'm sure when he hears how you've been behaving he'll thoroughly agree with what I'm doing,' said Mr Lenoir. 'Now, off with you!'

Poor George was propelled upstairs by Block, who was delighted to be punishing one of the children. As she came to the door of her room George shouted to the others, who were in Julian's room next door.

'Julian! Dick! Help me!'

Go to **163**.

168

George was hardly behind the sofa before Mr Lenoir entered the room and sat down at his desk. He switched on a lamp and began to look at some documents.

George couldn't think what in the world to do. It would be terrible to hide there for hours! What would the others think? They must be looking for her. She crouched there for nearly half an hour while Mr Lenoir worked. He gave a sudden yawn, then another one, and George's heart felt lighter. Perhaps he would have a nap. She could creep out then, and try to get into the secret passage.

Mr Lenoir yawned again. Then he pushed his papers aside and went to the sofa. He lay down on it and pulled the rug there over his knees, settling himself for a good sleep.

Soon the sound of rhythmic snores reached George's ears. She began to move very cautiously, squeezing out from behind the sofa. Then she stood up and started to press the panel. Unfortunately Timmy was waiting just the other side, and as soon as he heard George he started to whine and scratch at the panelling. George looked around at the sleeping man. Would he wake up?

*If you think Mr Lenoir wakes up, go to **161**.*
*If you think he sleeps on, go to **173**.*

169

Much to George's relief the door opened easily, and she slipped into the room and across to the cupboard. She flung open the door, and had a moment's surprise when she found that the cupboard was empty. Then she remembered that all Sooty's clothes had been taken to Julian's and Dick's room. She looked at the back of the cupboard to see if she could tell where the entrance to the passage was, but there was no sign of it. Unless you knew about it, you would never guess that the secret passage was there at all.

Swiftly she pressed the place in the panelling that opened the passage door, and Timmy came bounding out, wagging his tail with pleasure at seeing her.

'Sorry I've been so long, old chap,' she said, giving him a pat. 'Come on!'

George turned the door handle, but nothing happened. Block had come back and locked the door!

Go to **166**.

170

The footsteps stopped. George crouched in the chest hardly daring to breathe. Then she heard Mr Lenoir's voice.

'That sounded like a knock at the front door,' he said to himself. George heard him walk over to the big oak front door and open it, but of course no one was there. 'Funny,' said Mr Lenoir. 'I could have sworn I heard a knock. Oh, well, never mind.'

Go to **176**.

171

If you've arrived from **158**, *score* $\bigcirc$.

In the end George decided that it would be best to wait until Mr Lenoir left the room, even if it turned out to be a long wait.

George crouched in the dark, her hand on Timmy's collar. She had turned off her torch to save the battery, but a little bit of light filtered into the passage from the edge of the panel that moved. She could hear occasional noises from the study, and then, to her enormous relief, she heard Block's voice say, 'Mrs Lenoir is asking for you, sir. I believe she has mislaid a piece of jewellery.'

'Thank you, Block,' said Mr Lenoir. 'I'll come right away.'

George waited until she thought she heard Mr Lenoir leave the room, then she pushed the knob again.

Go to **160**.

172

At teatime the others went off to the playroom, wishing they didn't have to leave George. She felt very lonely when the others had gone. She was hungry, and she was very worried about Timmy. She longed desperately to escape from the house and go home to Kirrin Cottage.

The others sat down to tea feeling almost as miserable as George. The sight of a large chocolate cake did a certain amount to cheer them up, especially Dick, but everyone wished they could share it with George!

'Poor old George,' said Dick. 'I wish we could think of some way to get some food to her. This is your house, Sooty – can't you think of any way we could manage it?'

Sooty thought hard.

*If you think Sooty can think of a way to get food to George, go to **179**.*

*If you think he can't, go to **185**.*

173

Mr Lenoir muttered something under his breath and shifted on the sofa, but he didn't wake up. George turned back to the panelling with shaking hands, and started to press at it again. In her panic she had forgotten the right place, and she got more and more agitated as she searched for it. Timmy whined again, and George whispered to him as loudly as she dared.

'Sh, Timmy! I'll get you out of there as soon as I can.'

Timmy obviously settled down after that, because there was no more noise from the secret passage. George, who by this time was nearly frantic, moved to her left to try another piece of panelling, and tripped over the edge of the rug! She stumbled slightly and bumped against the back of the sofa.

*Go to **161**.*

174

Julian opened the passage door and looked down

the corridor. It was empty, so they all ran quickly along to the door. Sooty led them up a small flight of stairs just to the right of the passage door, and along another corridor, very like the one they had just left. At the end of the corridor he opened a door and led them in. It was a small room, but it was decorated in a much brighter, more comfortable way than any of the other rooms in the house. A sewing machine stood on a table on one side of the room, and there were two comfortable easy chairs, upholstered in yellow and white.

'What a pretty room!' exclaimed Anne.

'It's my mother's special room,' said Sooty. 'I think she comes up here to get away from my stepfather sometimes. Now, Dick, wrap a napkin around one of those pieces of cake while I open the window.'

Go to **177**.

175

'Here's what I plan to do, then,' said George. 'I'll use the rope ladder to get down on to the wall, go along it for some way, then jump down and creep back to the house. When everyone has gone to bed I'll get into the study again and see if I can rescue Timmy.'

'Right,' said Sooty. 'I'll open the side door for you. Good luck!'

Go to **181**.

If you've arrived from 170, score ♫.

George heard Mr Lenoir's footsteps crossing the hall, then silence. She gave a long sigh of relief, then lifted the lid of the chest and jumped out quickly. She dashed into the study and over to the panelling. But before she could even run her fingers over the smooth brown oak, she heard footsteps returning. Mr Lenoir was coming back! In a panic, poor George looked around for somewhere to hide. There was a large sofa against one wall. George crawled behind it, finding there was just enough room for her to crouch there without being seen.

Go to 168.

Sooty flung the window open and peered down. He could see the light shining from George's room, and knew that the curtains were open. He had been half afraid she might have drawn the curtains already, and wouldn't be able to see the cake.

Julian knotted a piece of string around the neatly wrapped cake, and handed it to Sooty. Leaning out of the window, Sooty lowered the cake carefully down until it was hanging just outside George's window. Nothing happened, so he started to swing the string to and fro gently, hoping George would notice the movement, but on the third swing the piece of cake fell out of the string and down on to the wall!

'Blast!' said Sooty. 'Can you wrap another piece, Dick? I'll try again.'

Go to **180**.

178

Just then there was a knock at the door.

'George! Are you awake?' came Julian's voice.

'Yes!' replied George. 'What's happening?'

'Block's gone to his room – Sarah says he's got a headache,' called Julian.

'Perhaps we can find some way of getting into Sooty's room and letting Timmy out,' suggested George.

'No, it's no good,' called Sooty. 'Block put the key on his keyring, which is attached to his belt. I saw him do it.'

Go to **175**.

179

Suddenly Sooty grinned, and his eyes sparkled with mischief.

'I know!' he exclaimed. 'There's a little room above George's – it's used as a sewing room by my mother sometimes. The window is directly above George's. If we wrap a piece of chocolate cake in a napkin, and tie a piece of string around it, we can lower it down to her!'

'What a good idea!' exclaimed Anne.

'I'll cut several slices of cake before Block comes to take it away,' said Sooty. 'I'm sure she's very hungry by now, so we'll try to give her more than one piece.'

Picking up the knife, he cut several large slices of the delicious gooey cake, then grabbed a handful of paper napkins.

'Right,' he said, taking a ball of string from one of the cupboards, 'come on!'

Go to **174**.

180

Dick wrapped another piece of cake, and Julian tied the string around it. Once again Sooty lowered it carefully out of the window and down the side of the house, but still nothing happened. He jiggled the string up and down to try to attract George's attention, but it was no good. A second piece of cake went tumbling down to join the first piece on the wall.

'I suppose the birds will eat it,' said Sooty, 'so somebody will have benefited. I wonder why George hasn't seen the cake? What can she be doing?'

Unknown to the others, George was curled up on the bed asleep. She was worn out with misery and rage, and she had dropped off. She didn't sleep for very long, but she never even saw the bits of cake that the others had tried to give her.

In the sewing room, Sooty closed the window. 'Come on,' he said. 'We'd better get back downstairs before Block wonders where we are.'

'Isn't there anything else we can do to get some food to George?' asked Julian. 'She must be starving.'

Go to **185**.

181

George sat down to wait until it was dark enough to climb down the rope ladder on to the town wall. Then she fastened it to the legs of her bed, threw it out of the open window, and scrambled down. The kitchen curtains were drawn, luckily, and she climbed on down to the wall without difficulty. She had put a torch in her pocket before she left her room, and now she switched it on and wondered what to do. She didn't want to run any risk of meeting Mr Lenoir. Perhaps the best thing to do would be to walk along the wall until she found a place where she could get off easily, and then make her way through the town back to Smuggler's Top. The height of the wall varied as it ran around the town, and in some places it was too high to jump off safely. She hadn't walked very far when she came to a place where the wall dipped to only about a metre above the ground. She looked down, wondering whether to get off there or to go on.

If you think George should get off there, go to **187**.
If you think she should go further, go to **193**.

182

George knew that Mr Barling's house was near the main street, so she carried on along the wall until she came to a part of the town that she knew, just beside the big arched town gateway. She had no trouble finding her way back to Smuggler's Top. The old house looked rather eerie in the failing light, and George gave a shiver. It looked like the sort of house that might be haunted! She ran quickly up the drive, and knocked on the little side door. Nothing happened, so George knocked again. Had something prevented Sooty from coming down to let her in?

If you think Sooty is there, go to **190**.
If you think he isn't, go to **197**.

183

The cobbled street went up to a T-junction, and George stopped and looked both ways, wondering which direction to take. To her left the road seemed to end in a blank wall about fifty metres away, but to her right it ran diagonally up the hill, and there were one or two shops on either side.

George thought that she could find her way back to Smuggler's Top from the middle of the town without any trouble. She had walked through the main shopping area every day with the others, and knew the route quite well, so she decided to take the right-hand road, as it seemed to lead up to the centre of the town. It was much wider than the little street she had come from, and there were quite a few people there. George hadn't gone very far when someone tapped her on the shoulder. She jumped out of her skin!

Go to **189**.

184

'What are we going to do?' asked George. 'I'll have to get Timmy tonight, or he'll be frantic. I think I'd better go and climb through my window again now, in case anyone comes along and finds that I've disappeared. I'll wait until everyone is asleep, then I'll slip out of the window again. Could you let me in, Sooty? Then we can go to the study, open the secret way, and I can find Timmy.'

'I'll come and knock at your door when it's quiet,' promised Sooty. 'You go back to your room now.

We've got to go down and say hello to your father, and afterwards we'll come and tell you what he said.'

George made her way out of the house, along the wall and back to her bedroom, where she sat on the bed, feeling rather lonely. After what seemed like hours there was a tap on her door.

'It's me!' called Julian. 'We've seen Uncle Quentin, and he's frightfully annoyed with you for misbehaving. He said you were to be locked up for the whole of tomorrow, too, if you don't apologise.'

'Well, I'm jolly well not going to!' said George furiously. 'Good night!'

'Good night,' called Julian. 'Sleep well!'

Go to **192**.

185

If you've arrived from **180**, *score* ◁ ◁ ◁ ◁.

Sooty shook his head. 'It's no use,' he said. 'I'm afraid poor old George will have to do without for the time being.'

George lay on her bed, staring unhappily at the ceiling. In a while she got up and went over to the window. It looked down over the steep hillside, and below was the wide wall that ran around the town. George knew that she couldn't jump down to the wall. She might roll off it and fall straight down to the marsh below. Then she suddenly remembered something. In her suitcase, under the bed, was the rope ladder they used every morning to climb down into the catacombs!

Originally it had been kept in Mary's room, but they had been afraid that Block might find it while he was cleaning the room, so they had put it in George's case, which had a lock, for safe keeping. If she lowered it out of the window, she might be able to climb down on to the wall!

Go to **178**.

186

If you've arrived from **191**, *score* ◠⊃ .

Sooty vanished. He was soon back, looking puzzled.

'Block's in bed!' he said. 'I could see the shape of his body and the dark patch of his head. Are there *two* Blocks, then? Whatever does it mean?'

It was all very puzzling – especially to George, who had felt certain it was Block she had seen talking to Mr Barling. The others weren't so certain, especially since George admitted she hadn't seen the man's face.

'Is my father here yet?' asked George suddenly. 'Wasn't he supposed to get here this evening?'

'Yes, he arrived a couple of hours ago,' answered Sooty.

Go to **184**.

George decided to get off the wall there. After all, she might not come to another good place for a long time. She jumped to the ground and set off up a narrow cobbled street towards the middle of Castaway.

The street ran uphill for a short way, then curved to the left. There were no shops in that part of the town, only houses. All the curtains were drawn, but quite a lot of light still came from the windows, and George was able to find her way without using her torch. There were still a few people about, and one or two of them gave her rather curious looks, wondering what a girl of her age was doing wandering around alone in the dark.

Go to **183**.

188

Surely that was Block in there? He had his back to the window, but George could have sworn it was Block! The same thick dark hair, the same shoulders! Who was he talking to? George moved a little further along the wall – and got another shock. Block was talking to Mr Barling!

But wait a minute – how could it be Block? Block was deaf, and the man talking to Mr Barling obviously wasn't. He was clearly listening to what Mr Barling said, and replying. From time to time he

nodded his head in agreement with the other man.

'If only he'd turn around I'd know for certain whether it's Block or not,' said George to herself. 'Yet it can't be Block – he's supposed to be lying down with a headache! It's all very peculiar. I must get back to Smuggler's Top as quickly as I can and tell the others.'

Go to **182**.

189

George swung around, her heart thumping with fright. She expected to see Mr Lenoir, or Block, or even Mrs Lenoir, but it was a strange man who stood there.

'I'm sorry if I startled you,' said the man, 'but is this your torch? It fell out of your pocket as you walked along.'

George gave a huge sigh of relief and smiled at the man.

'Yes, it is,' she said, taking it from him and turning it on to make sure it was still working. 'Thank you very much. I wonder – could you please tell me how to get to the middle of Castaway? I'm a bit lost.'

The man gave a laugh.

'It's a confusing place, isn't it?' he answered. 'I'm afraid I can't help you. I only moved here two weeks ago, and I still haven't learnt my way around. Sorry!'

Go to **196**.

190

The door swung open and Sooty pulled her in, his finger to his lips. Silently they tiptoed past the study, across the hall, and up to Julian's bedroom, where the others were waiting. Sooty had raided the larder, and sandwiches, cakes and a cold pie were spread out on a tray. George sat down and started to eat. She was absolutely starving! In between bites she told them all about seeing the man who looked like Block in Mr Barling's house.

'It *can't* have been Block,' said Sooty. 'While I was raiding the larder I heard Sarah telling my mother that Block had such a bad headache he'd probably stay in bed until morning.'

'Well, I'm certain it was him,' said George. 'Yet how can it have been? It's all very, very odd.'

'I tell you what,' said Sooty, jumping to his feet, 'I'll go and see if Block is in bed. If he is, then we'll know it wasn't him you saw, George.'

Go to **186**.

191

If you've arrived from **202**, *score* ⊂⃝:

George opened the door of Julian's room a crack and looked in. She didn't want to walk straight in, in case she met Sarah or Mr Lenoir.

'Come on in, George,' said Julian's voice. 'There's nobody here but us.'

They were all sitting on the floor, and on the bed were plates of sandwiches, cake and a cold pork pie.

'Here's your supper, George,' said Anne. 'You must be starving!'

George sat down and started to eat. Between mouthfuls she told the others about seeing the man who looked like Block in Mr Barling's house.

'It *can't* have been Block,' said Sooty. 'While I was raiding the larder I heard Sarah telling my mother that Block had such a terrible headache he'd probably stay in bed until morning.'

'Well, it certainly looked like him,' said George, 'but it couldn't have been! It's all very, very odd.'

'I tell you what,' said Sooty, jumping up. 'I'll go and see if Block is in bed. If he is, we'll know it wasn't him you saw, George.'

Go to **186**.

192

George lay on her bed, thinking about the man she had seen in Mr Barling's house, but before long her eyes closed, and soon she was fast asleep, worn out after the worries and excitements of the day.

At midnight she awoke with a jump. Someone was knocking softly on her door.

'Is that you, Sooty?' she called, but there was no reply.

'Sooty, is that you?' she called again.

If you think it's Sooty at the door, go to **198**.
If you think it's someone else, go to **204**.

193

If you've arrived from **196**, *score* ◯◁ ◯◁ ◯◁ ◯◁.

George decided to keep on going, and she moved along the broad, uneven top of the old wall, shining her torch in front of her. The wall ran around some stables, then around the back of some shops, then past several old houses. George could look into the windows where the curtains hadn't been drawn. She saw families having supper, people watching television, and some rooms that were empty, even though the lights were on. Then she came to a very large house. The wall ran close against it, and on the other side of the wall the hill dropped steeply into the marsh far below.

George looked in at the lighted window as she passed, and got a great surprise!

Go to **188**.

194

If you've arrived from **199**, *score* ⌒.

'There's only one thing to do, George,' said Sooty. 'I'll have to creep into my old bedroom – the one your father's sleeping in – and try to get into the secret way from the entrance in my cupboard. Then I can find Timmy and bring him out to you. We'll just have to hope that your father is too tired to wake up if I make any noise!'

'Oh, Sooty!' exclaimed George. 'You *are* a good friend. Are you sure you don't want me to do it?'

Sooty shook his head. 'I know the way up and down that passage better than you do.'

They tiptoed through the dark house, up the stairs to the big oak door. Just as Sooty was about to open it, George shook his arm.

'Sooty, if you open that door the buzzer will go off in your room and wake my father!' she whispered.

Go to **200**.

195

Sooty was unable to stay awake any longer. His head slipped to one side, to rest against the wall, and his body relaxed into a half-lying position. For a while there was no sound in the room except regular breathing. However, about ten minutes later something strange happened. There was a creaking noise from the window seat. Had Sooty been awake, he would have heard it, but he was fast asleep, worn out after a difficult day.

Go to **206**.

196

The man walked off, and George went on up the road. It continued to run uphill for a little way, then began to curve downwards. George looked for a turning that would take her uphill, but there weren't any to be seen. The road continued to lead her down the hill again, and suddenly she realised that she was back at the wall.

'Oh, bother!' she muttered crossly. 'This is the last place I want to be.' She stood still, trying to decide what to do. If she retraced her steps she would probably get lost again, so the best thing would be to get back on to the wall and have a look around – perhaps when she was a bit higher up she would be able to see where she was. It was impossible to see anything but houses from the road. She walked along the side of the wall for a way, until she came to a place where she could scramble back on to it. For a moment she wondered whether she would be better off going back to the house by the rope ladder.

Go to **193**.

197

George knocked a third time, and when nothing happened she tried the door handle. Much to her surprise the door swung open. She slipped into the house, closing the door behind her, then tiptoed past the study and across the hall. She ran up the staircase as fast as she could, through the big oak door and down the passage. All the doors were closed, and for a moment she wondered whether to try the door of Sooty's room to see if it had been left open. Her hand was on the knob when she remembered that her father was supposed to be arriving that day, and he might well be in the room. She took her hand off the door knob and looked at the other doors. Were the others in Julian and Dick's room, or in the playroom?

If you think George should go to Julian's room, go to **191**.
If you think she should go to the playroom, go to **202**.

198

'Yes, it is,' replied Sooty. 'Come on. I'm going downstairs to wait by the side door.'

George picked up her torch, let down the rope ladder, and was soon hurrying along the wall. She jumped to the ground and made her way to the side door of the house. Sooty was there, and she slipped in thankfully.

'Come on,' she said impatiently to Sooty.

They went to the study door, and Sooty turned the handle. It was locked!

'We should have remembered that it might be locked,' said George in despair. 'Oh, blow, blow, blow! What are we going to do now?'

Go to **194**.

199

'Well, I wish you luck,' replied Mary. 'I'm going back to bed.'

'Thanks, Mary,' said George.

She let down the rope ladder and was soon hurrying along the wall. Jumping to the ground, she made her way around the house to the side door, where Sooty was waiting. He closed the door behind her, and they made their way to the study. Sooty tried the handle. The door was locked!

'We should have thought of that,' said George in despair. 'Oh, blow, blow, blow! What are we going to do now?'

Go to **194**.

200

'Idiot!' answered Sooty. 'I disconnected the buzzer as soon as I knew that your father would be using my room.'

He opened the door, and they crept up the passage to Sooty's old room. The door was closed.

'You go into Mary's room and wait,' Sooty whispered to George. 'I'll go and find Timmy.'

George crept into the room next door, where Anne and Mary were fast asleep. She left the door open so that she could hear Sooty when he came back, and sat down on the end of Anne's bed.

Go to **203**.

201

The intruder put George's father into the window seat. What he had done to poor George's father to make him unable to struggle, Sooty didn't know. He only knew that Uncle Quentin didn't seem to be able to help himself at all.

Suddenly Sooty found his voice. 'Hey!' he yelled. 'What are you doing?'

He remembered his torch, and switched it on. He saw a face he knew, and cried out in surprise: 'Mr Barling!'

Then someone hit him a hard blow on the head and he remembered nothing more. He didn't know that he, too, was lifted into the window seat, nor did he know that the intruder followed him down into the darkness.

Go to **205**.

202

George decided to try the playroom first. She opened the door cautiously and looked in. The room appeared to be empty, and George was just about to shut the door and go to the boys' room when she heard the door at the end of the passage being opened. She shot across the room and into the big cupboard, pulling the doors closed just as the playroom door opened. Through the gap between the doors George could see Sarah putting clean plates and knives and forks on the table for breakfast the next morning. Then she bustled out, and George forced herself to wait several minutes before opening the cupboard doors. She crossed the corridor to Julian's and Dick's room.

Go to **191**.

Sooty slipped into the room where George's father lay. He was able to avoid every creaking board, because he knew where they were, and he made his way to a big chair, meaning to hide behind it until he was certain that George's father was sound asleep.

For some time the man in the bed tossed and turned. Uncle Quentin was tired after his long journey, but his mind had been stimulated by his talk with Mr Lenoir. He moved restlessly, muttering occasionally, and Sooty began to feel that he would never be sound asleep. Then Sooty began to grow sleepy himself. His eyelids drooped, no matter how hard he tried to keep them open, and his head fell forwards.

If you think Sooty falls asleep, go to **195**.
If you think he manages to stay awake, go to **208**.

204

'It's me, Mary,' came the reply. 'Sooty's gone downstairs to the side door already. He asked me to come to tell you he'll be waiting for you.'

'Right,' said George, looking around for her torch.

'Oh, George, do be careful,' said Mary. 'Your father will be so angry if he catches you. He's very cross with you anyway, for being so much trouble to my father.'

'I'm not afraid of what my father might say,' said George stoutly. 'I just want to get Timmy out of that dreadful tunnel. The trouble is, if Sooty and I get caught, he'll be in far worse trouble than I shall. Your father is even fiercer than mine.'

'They're rather alike,' said Mary, 'both with dreadful tempers, both doing scientific experiments that none of us can understand.'

'Let's just hope we don't get caught!' said George fervently.

Go to **199**.

205

George, awake in the next room, suddenly heard Sooty's voice crying out: 'Hey. What are you doing?' And then she heard the next cry: 'Mr Barling!'

George was extremely startled. What was going on next door? She fumbled about for her torch, then tiptoed to the door, trembling from head to foot. She shone her torch and saw that the door of Sooty's room was ajar, just as Sooty had left it. She listened, but there was absolutely no sound. She had heard a small bumping noise after Sooty's last cry, but she didn't know what it was.

She tiptoed along the passage and stuck her head around the door of Sooty's room, shining her torch in front of her. The torch flashed over the bed, and to George's intense surprise the bed was empty! The room was empty! Whatever had been happening?

She sat down on the window seat, puzzled and scared, and tried to decide the best thing to do. In her fright she had forgotten about poor Timmy, still shut in the secret passage, but now she wondered whether it would be best to try to get him out right away. Or should she wait and see if anything else happened?

If you think she should try to find Timmy, go to **210**.
If you think she should wait and see, go to **216**.

206

The creaking noise went on. There are always odd noises in an old house at night. Furniture and floorboards creak, and sometimes mice can be heard squeaking behind the wainscot, but the noise that was coming from the window seat was different from the usual night-time sounds of Smuggler's Top. Sooty's head suddenly jerked up, and he sat up cautiously, his heart pounding. He had woken with a terrible jump, and knew that there had been a strange noise somewhere in the room. He strained his eyes, trying to get accustomed to the dark again. Then he heard a creaking noise that seemed to come from the window. The curtains were open, and the window showed as a square of grey in the blackness of the room. As he stared, Sooty saw something that made him go cold.

Go to **211**.

George lay under the bed, shivering, for a little while longer. Then she rolled out from under the bed, out of Sooty's room and down the passage, then across the landing to the boys' room.

Julian and Dick were awake, waiting for Sooty to come in with Timmy and George.

But only George arrived. A scared George, who had a very strange story to tell. The boys listened to her in astonishment. Uncle Quentin and Sooty gone! Someone creeping into the room and fiddling with the window seat! What did it all mean?

Julian got out of bed. 'I think we'd better come along to Uncle Quentin's room with you right now and have a look around. This is beginning to sound very serious.'

'Wouldn't it be better to go and wake Mr Lenoir first? Perhaps he could get in touch with the police or something,' suggested Dick.

If you agree with Julian, go to **213**.
If you agree with Dick, go to **219**.

Sooty pinched himself, then recited in his head a few multiplication tables, trying to stop himself from falling asleep. At last George's father grew quiet and peaceful. Sooty moved cautiously out from behind the chair. Then suddenly something startled him.

He heard a sound, over by the window. It was a very small sound, like a door creaking slightly. The night was rather dark, but the window, its curtains drawn back, could easily be seen as a square of grey. Sooty looked at it. Was someone opening the window? No. The window wasn't moving, but something odd was happening underneath it!

Go to **211**.

209

Julian went to the cupboard and opened it. He pushed the clothes aside and groped for the little iron handle that pulled out the stone at the back. It was gone! Someone had removed it, and now there was no way of getting into the secret passage from Sooty's room!

'Well, the midnight visitor, whoever he was, didn't get in and out of the room that way,' said Julian.

'I'm sure Mr Lenoir is at the bottom of all this,' said Dick suddenly. 'And Block as well, I expect. He and Mr Lenoir are probably hand in glove in whatever is going on.'

'So that means we can't tell him what's happened,' said Anne, looking scared. 'We can't tell Mrs Lenoir, either, because she's bound to tell her husband!'

Go to **212**.

210

The thought of poor Timmy waiting patiently in the passage made George decide to try to get him out. She slid off the window seat and went over to the big cupboard. Opening the doors, she saw that it was full of clothes belonging to her father.

Father must be here somewhere, thought George. All his clothes are here, and he would hardly have gone out in his dressing-gown and pyjamas. Perhaps he went to the bathroom. That wouldn't explain Sooty crying out, though. Oh dear, this is all *very* peculiar.

George parted the clothes to reach for the handle that opened the secret passage.

Go to **216**.

211

If you've arrived from **206**, *score* ⌢.

The top of the window seat was slowly moving upwards! Sooty was puzzled. He didn't know it could be moved like that; it had always been screwed down. He stared at the moving lid. There must be someone inside, lifting it up . . . At last the lid was fully open, and a big figure climbed silently out. Sooty was terrified, unable to move. He watched as the figure crossed the room to the bed. The figure made a quick movement, and there was a stifled sound from George's father. Sooty guessed he had been gagged. Then the intruder lifted the limp body from the bed and went to the window seat.

Go to **201**.

212

'I think we should all go back to bed,' said Julian, with a cheerfulness that he didn't really feel. 'Perhaps Uncle Quentin and Sooty will have turned up by the morning. If they haven't, we'll *have* to tell Mr Lenoir. He'll probably send for the police. Now, George, you'd better go and sleep with Mary and Anne, and Dick and I will sleep here in Sooty's old room. I should lock your door, to be on the safe side.'

George, Anne and Mary went back to the girls' room and were soon settled down for what was left of the night. George slept on a small sofa, covered with a blanket from Mary's bed.

Go to **218**.

213

If you've arrived from **219**, *score* ⌒ꜱ.

Julian shook his head. 'There may be some simple

explanation of what's going on,' he said, 'though I must say I doubt it! Still, we don't want to wake Mr Lenoir in the middle of the night unless we're sure something's happened to Sooty and Uncle Quentin. Come on.'

Dick went and woke Mary and Anne, then they all went into Sooty's old room, from which he and Uncle Quentin had so strangely vanished. Julian drew the curtains and turned on the light, which made them feel better. They looked around the room, but all they could see was the rumpled bed, and Sooty's torch, lying on the floor.

'Why should Sooty call out Mr Barling's name?' wondered George. 'Unless – do you think Mr Barling came up the secret passage to do some dirty work in this house, got caught by Father and

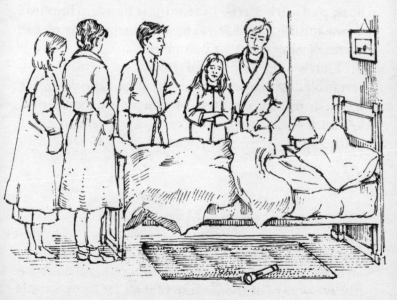

Sooty, and took them back with him, because they saw him?'

'I suppose that might be what happened,' said Julian doubtfully. 'Let's have a look at the entrance to the secret passage.'

Go to **209**.

214

'I think it might be a good idea,' said Julian. 'Quick, get under the bed!'

The two boys rolled under the bed. Julian lifted up the edge of the valance so that he could see whoever came in. The door swung open, and Block appeared with a tray of tea in his hands. He put it down on the bedside table and walked out of the room, closing the door behind him.

'That's very odd,' said Julian, as he and Dick scrambled out from under the bed. 'Block didn't seem to be the slightest bit surprised that Uncle Quentin wasn't here!'

Go to **220**.

215

'Listen, Mr Lenoir,' Julian said boldly, 'some very strange things have been going on here, and we believe you're at the bottom of it all.'

'Go on, Julian,' Mary urged through her tears. 'Tell him.'

'We know things about Block.' Julian stood in front of Mr Lenoir with his fists clenched. 'And we think you and he . . .'

'Be quiet!' Mr Lenoir raged at him. 'I won't hear any more of your insane childish ravings.'

Go to **225**.

216

If you've arrived from **210**, *score* ☖.

Suddenly George heard a faint sound from the corridor. As fast as lightning she slipped under the bed. Someone was creeping down the long passage and into the room. George lay on the floor, lifting the valance a little to try to see who it was.

Someone came in at the door and stopped for a moment, as if he were looking around the room. Then he crept over to the window seat. George could see a figure outlined against the grey square of the window.

As she watched, the figure bent over the window seat. He didn't use a torch, but George heard some curious sounds. First came the sound of his fingers tapping on the closed lid of the seat, then the clink of something metallic, and a very faint squeaking. George couldn't imagine what the man – if it was a man – was doing.

For about five minutes the mysterious person worked away in the darkness. Then, as quietly as he had come, he went away. George couldn't help wondering if it could be Block. It was much too dark for her to be able to see his face, but he had once given a little cough exactly like Block so often gave.

Go to **207**.

217

'Barling knows all the secret passages and ins and outs of this house,' Mr Lenoir went on, 'better than I do.'

The children stared at him, adjusting their minds to believing that he was innocent after all.

'I'm going to talk to Block.' Mr Lenoir got up. 'We'll see if he knows anything about this mystery.'

Go to **221**.

218

In the morning George woke up first. She lay on the sofa thinking over the odd things that had happened the night before, and worrying about Timmy. It seemed a very long time since she had last seen him.

In the room next door Julian and Dick were also awake, and also puzzling over the night's events. Suddenly Julian heard the clink of china. Someone was coming along the corridor, carrying a tray.

'Do you think that's Block or Sarah?' hissed Dick. 'Perhaps we should hide.'

'It's probably Sarah,' said Julian. 'She'll think it's odd that Uncle Quentin isn't here, won't she? Though I'm certain she's not mixed up in whatever is going on at Smuggler's Top.'

'Ought we to hide,' suggested Dick, 'just in case it's Block?'

If you think they should hide, go to **214**.
If you think they should stay in bed, go to **224**.

219

George and Julian looked at Dick.

'You must be mad!' said George rather crossly. 'You know what Mr Lenoir is like. If we wake him up in the middle of the night to tell him that his stepson has disappeared, together with his guest, he'll never believe us. He'll just get into a furious temper and we'll probably *all* be locked in our rooms tomorrow.'

'If we take him to Sooty's old room and show him that Uncle Quentin isn't there – and that Sooty isn't in bed in our room – he'll know we're telling the truth. It sounds to me as if all this is really a job for the police,' insisted Dick.

'Pooh!' said George scornfully. 'We've solved plenty of mysteries without any help from the police!'

'What do you think, Julian?' asked Dick. 'Shall we go to Mr Lenoir?'

Go to **213**.

Dick looked at Julian.

'That means that Block *is* involved in Uncle Quentin's disappearance!' he said. 'Hold on a minute – if Block knew that Uncle Quentin wasn't here, why did he bring up the tea?'

'That's obvious,' replied Julian. 'If Sarah got a tray of tea ready, and asked Block to bring it up, he could hardly tell her that Uncle Quentin wasn't in his room, could he?'

'No,' said Dick, 'but perhaps Block just thought Uncle Quentin had gone to have a wash.'

'That's a possibility,' answered Julian. 'After all, we've still got no real proof that Block is up to anything sinister.'

They decided to take the tea-tray into the girls' room, where they shared the tea, taking it in turns to drink from the same cup.

Presently Block appeared. He stared angrily at George. He had thought she was locked in her own room – and here she was in Mary's room, drinking tea.

Go to **227**.

Go to **227**.

221

At breakfast in the playroom, Julian said, 'It's up to us to solve the mystery. Let's start by exploring your father's room, George. If Mr Barling kidnapped

Uncle Quentin and Sooty, there must be another secret way out of there.'

'I've just remembered!' George knocked over her orange juice in excitement. 'I heard Sooty yell out: "Mr Barling!"'

'Could they be hidden in Mr Barling's house?' Anne asked.

'Brilliant!' Julian shouted. 'Of course. I'm going down there to find out.'

'I'm coming too,' George insisted.

'No, it's too dangerous. Only Dick comes with me. You girls stay here.'

'Beast!' George threw a piece of toast at him. 'I'm as good as any boy. But see if I care. I've got plans of my own.'

Go to **228**.

222

'Tell me what happened,' Mrs Lenoir begged in anguish.

'Well, it's true. Uncle Quentin and Sooty have disappeared,' Julian said cautiously. 'But they'll probably turn up.'

'You're keeping back something, Julian.' Mr Lenoir was watching him sharply. 'I insist that you tell me everything.'

'You may not like it,' Julian said.

'Don't play games with me, boy.' The tip of Mr

Lenoir's nose was white with anger. 'What are you hiding?'

'You're the one who's keeping secrets,' Julian blurted out before he could stop himself.

No one spoke. Mr Lenoir stared in amazement. 'What are you talking about?'

Hearing a noise outside the door, Julian opened it. Block stood there.

Go to **226**.

223

If you've arrived from **230**, *score* ◯◁.

Mr Lenoir sat behind his cluttered desk. Mrs Lenoir and Mary were still tearful and anxious.

'Don't worry, children.' Mr Lenoir seemed kinder than before. 'We'll get to the bottom of this. But if Pierre and George's father don't return soon, I must know what to tell the police when they come.'

It was extraordinary. Mr Lenoir was suddenly much nicer and more reasonable. 'I think I know who's behind this,' he said. 'What's your information, Julian?'

'Well, sir.' Julian was pleased to be treated as an equal. 'This is a strange house, with lots of peculiar things going on.'

'Like?'

'Like the signalling from the tower, for a start.'

'Signalling?' Mr Lenoir seemed genuinely astonished, so Julian told him how they had seen the

flashes and the pinpricks of light across the marsh from the sea, and had followed the signaller to Block's room.

'Block has nothing to do with this, I swear,' Mr Lenoir told them.

'Then who?'

'*Mr Barling.*'

Go to **217**.

224

The door opened and Sarah came in, carrying a tray with a pot of tea on it. She gaped at the boys in surprise.

'Where's your uncle? Why are you here?' she asked.

'Oh . . . er . . . we'll explain later,' said Julian. 'Please leave the tea, Sarah.'

'Yes, but where's your uncle?' asked Sarah again. 'Is he in your room?'

'Well, you could always go and have a look,' said Dick, hoping Sarah would go away.

She put down the tray of tea and left the room, looking very puzzled. Dick and Julian carried the tea next door to the girls, who were all awake, and they took it in turns to drink from one cup.

Presently Block came in. He stared angrily at George. He had thought she was locked in her own room – and here she was in Mary's room, drinking tea!

Go to **227**.

225

Julian's face was stricken. He turned and rushed from the room. Anne stayed with poor Mary, but George and Dick followed Julian along the passage and down the stairs. They heard him slam the side door, and found him outside on a low wall overlooking the cliff. George put her arm around him.

'Leave me alone!'

She knew why he wouldn't look at her. It wasn't being called insane that he had minded. It was being called childish.

Go to **230**.

'Snooping,' Julian said. 'I'm not saying anything in front of him.'

'He's deaf, poor fellow.'

'Is he really? We don't trust him. We hate him.'

Julian and Block glared at each other.

'This is too much,' Mr Lenoir was struggling to control his temper. 'You children have caused nothing but trouble. You disobey me. You insult my servant, whom I've known for years. Julian – I order you to tell me what this is all about.'

'I'd rather tell it to the police,' Julian said stubbornly.

'All right.' Mr Lenoir gave in. 'Go away, Block. Everyone else, come down to my study.'

Go to **223**.

If you've arrived from **220**, *score* ⌁.

'How did you get out?' he demanded furiously. 'I'll tell Mr Lenoir.'

'Shut up,' said Julian. 'Don't speak to my cousin like that. Clear out, Block.'

Whether Block heard or not, he didn't go.

Julian faced him determinedly. 'We think you're mixed up in this rotten business. The police will want to talk to you, Block. Now clear out!'

Block gave him an evil look and shambled out. 'I shall go to Mr Lenoir.'

In a few minutes Mary's parents came to her room.

'What's all this?' Mr Lenoir asked. 'Block came to me with an extraordinary tale that George's father has disappeared, and . . .'

'And so has Sooty!' Mary wailed. 'Sooty's gone too!'

Mrs Lenoir gave a cry. 'Sooty gone? What do you mean?'

'Let me tell it, Mary,' Julian said quickly, although he wasn't sure what he was going to say. He wanted to accuse Mr Lenoir of being at the bottom of the sinister plot – but was it too soon?

*If you think Julian should accuse Mr Lenoir, go to **215**.*
*If you think he should hold back, go to **222**.*

228

Julian and Dick went down the hill to Mr Barling's large house and knocked on the heavy oak front door. They had invented a story about collecting for the Scouts, to try to get inside.

While they waited, they looked up Castaway Hill to where the round tower of Smuggler's Top stood high against a windy sky.

'No wonder he uses the tower for signalling,' Dick said. 'Lights wouldn't be seen by the ships from down here.'

Julian knocked again. The windows were shut, the house was quiet. 'Isn't anyone going to answer the door?'

If you think someone answers the door, go to 234.
If not, go to 240.

229

Meanwhile, the three girls were alone in the playroom.

'Well,' George said to Anne, 'I don't suppose Mr Barling will let them in anyway.'

'I want Sooty,' Mary said miserably.

'So do I. And I want my Timmy. Look, I've got some investigating to do, so why don't you and Anne wait here. If anyone comes looking for Julian or Dick or me, make up some story – all right?'

Go to 231.

230

'If Mr Lenoir doesn't want to talk to us,' George brooded, 'what can we do?'

'Write him a letter,' Dick suggested.

'Make an anonymous phone call,' Julian grunted. 'I just want to tell him what I think of him.'

'George! Boys!' Mary was leaning out of a window above them. 'My father wants to talk to everyone in his study.'

'Now's your chance, then,' George said grimly.

Go to **223**.

231

George slipped into Uncle Quentin's room to see if there might be another secret passage Sooty didn't know about. She tapped the walls and turned back the carpet to examine every bit of floor. Nothing. She was just going out when she noticed something on the floor by the window. It glinted like a small jewel. An ear-ring, perhaps?

If you think it is an ear-ring, go to **236**.
If you think it's something else, go to **242**.

232

She had taken out almost all the screws when there was a pounding on the door and Julian shouted, 'George! We're back. Let us in!'

She unlocked the door, and the boys came in with Anne and Mary.

'Did you see Mr Barling?' she asked.

'He's gone away,' Julian said. 'The house is shut up. What on earth are you doing, George?'

'Playing the piano,' she joked, for everyone could see she was unscrewing the top of the seat.

'I'll finish it.' Dick held out his hand for the screwdriver.

'It's my job. Girls are as good as boys, I told you.'

George took out the last screw and lifted the lid of the window seat.

Everyone peered inside, half afraid of what they would see.

'I bet it's empty,' Anne said.

*If you think Anne is right, go to **238**.*
*If you think they find something, go to **244**.*

233

'Wait a sec,' Julian said. 'We don't want anyone to come in while we're going down. Dick, you go and see what Mr Lenoir is doing. I'll check on that crafty Block.'

The study door was ajar. When Dick looked in, Mr Lenoir was writing at his desk.

'Go away and don't bother me,' he said in his grumpy way. 'I've got to finish some important letters in time to get them in the post.'

Julian looked in the kitchen and the pantry and the staff sitting-room without finding Block. Finally, he crept up the stairs to the top bedroom, crouched down and peered through the keyhole.

Block was in bed again. He was a glutton for sleep. In the faint light through the drawn curtains, Julian could see the lumpy mound of his body and the dark shape of his head.

He sped back to the others. 'Block's safe for a bit. What about Mr Lenoir?'

'He's writing letters,' Dick said.

'Let's go down the hole, then. I can't wait to explore.'

'Hang on.' Dick caught his arm. 'Mr Lenoir is going out soon to the post-box. Shouldn't we wait until he's gone?'

If you think they should wait, go to **239**.
If you think they should go down now, go to **243**.

234

At last a woman opened the door, wearing a jacket and a headscarf.

'What do you boys want?' she asked. 'I'm late finishing work already, and I've got to get to the shops before I go home.'

'Well, we . . . er,' Julian began. Drat. They ought to have a collecting box or something.

'Sorry, I can't wait.' The woman locked the door and hurried to where her bicycle leaned against the fence, then she rode quickly away towards the shops.

Go to **237**.

'Only one way to find out,' Julian said. They all followed him to the room that Sooty had been sharing with the two boys. 'If the shirt's not there, we'll know.'

Mary rummaged in the cupboard among the three boys' clothes.

'I can't see it, I . . . no, look, here it is, Sooty's blue shirt, the only one he has.'

They compared it with the scrap of cloth. It didn't match.

'So much for your memory, George,' Dick said.

'We can't all be geniuses like you. Come on, we're wasting time,' replied George. 'Let's go back and examine the seat again. We might find something else.'

Go to **238**.

Go to **238**.

236

She bent to pick it up. It was the missing one of a pair of ear-rings that Sarah had worn on her last evening out. Sarah had offered to bake a cake for anyone who found it. Hurray! George would choose a chocolate cake for tea tomorrow. With fudge icing. So her careful search of the room that used to be

Sooty's wasn't entirely wasted. As she put it in her pocket, she saw something else near the window.

Go to **242**.

237

'Let's go after her,' Julian said. 'Make up some story – say our mother is an old family friend – anything to get her to come back and let us inside.'

The road took a curve, and they ran across a rocky meadow to cut the woman off. Dick stumbled into a rabbit hole.

'Oh . . . ow, my foot!'

By the time he got up and limped on again, they reached the road too late, and saw the bicycle sailing fast downhill into the crowded market place.

'Blow!' Julian said. 'Come on, let's go back and have a look around.'

Go to **240**.

238

If you've arrived from **235**, *score* ◁ ◁:

They could find nothing. George even got inside the empty seat and stamped on the bottom.

Suddenly there was a grinding *crunch*, and the floor of the window seat dropped down like a trap-door on a hinge.

'Help!' George clutched at the top of the seat and

hung on as her feet swung down into space. She kicked about frantically, and with the boys' help managed to pull herself up to safety.

As soon as her feet were on the floor, she turned and, with the others, peered down into a straight-sided, yawning hole. The light from the window showed that it was about two metres deep and opened out at the bottom into what looked like a passage.

'One of the tunnels that criss-cross everywhere under this old hill,' Julian said. 'I wonder if Sooty knew? It might even lead from here to Mr Barling's house, and that's how . . .'

'Let's go down and find Sooty,' Mary said eagerly.

'And Timmy,' George said. 'Come on, everyone, we might even find my father.'

Go to **233**.

239

They looked out of the window to see when Mr Lenoir would come out of the house with his hat and stick and set off for the post-box a short distance along the road.

They waited and waited. Eventually, Dick went downstairs and sneaked a look into the study. Mr Lenoir glanced up and saw him.

'Oh, er . . . er, hello,' Dick stammered. 'Letters all finished, sir?'

'Yes.' Mr Lenoir was putting on stamps.

'So you'll be going out to enjoy some fresh air?'

'I've got so much to do. Tell you what, boy. Run down with these to the post-box, would you? That would be a big help.'

Dick took the letters and sped down the hill. On the way back, he saw the others at the bedroom window. He waved, but they just looked puzzled.

'No luck,' he panted when he got back upstairs. 'He's not going out.'

Go to **243**.

240

If you've arrived from **237**, *score* ◁◁ ◁◁.

They knocked again and rang the bell, in case Mr Barling was at home. No answer. They went round to the back and were startled to see a man's head appear suddenly above a line of bushes.

'Hello, young lads.' He seemed friendly. 'Lost a ball or something?'

'We're looking for Mr Barling.'

'He's away on holiday,' said the gardener, who was working on the flower-beds next door. 'Drove off this morning. Don't know when he'll be back.'

'Oh.' Julian and Dick looked at each other blankly. 'Was anyone with him in the car – a man, or a boy, perhaps?'

The gardener scratched his head. 'I don't bother about other people's business. But no. He was alone.'

Alone, without his captives? Where were they? Why had he kidnapped Uncle Quentin? If Mr Lenoir knew the answer, he was keeping it dark. The mystery and crisis were deepening. Julian and Dick walked back up to Smuggler's Top in puzzled silence.

Go to **229**.

241

Then they heard the sound of low voices, and the light of a lantern shone dimly into the cave. Two men came out of the tunnel. One was thin and tall. The other – surely the other was Block!

But Block was asleep in bed. Julian had seen him there. How had he got out of the house so quickly and into these tunnels?

When the men had crossed the cave and the light of their lantern had faded down another tunnel, Anne whispered, 'The tall man looked like Mr Barling – long and skinny.'

'But Mr Barling's gone away,' Dick said.

'He might have sneaked back,' said George. 'And the other man was either Block, or his exact double.'

'One Block is bad enough,' Dick said. 'Let alone two. Come on, let's follow them. They might lead us to Sooty and Uncle Quentin.'

'No,' Julian said definitely. 'We could lose them, and lose ourselves in this maze of tunnels. Sooty said they run for miles, and criss-cross and go round and up and down – even down to the marsh.

If we got lost, what help would that be to Uncle Quentin and Sooty?'

'And my Timmy,' George said sadly. 'Oh, why doesn't he bark, wherever he is? I used to scold him for barking at people like the postman and the milkman. Now I'd give anything to hear just one good old Timmy bark!'

Go to **245**.

Go to **245**.

242

If you've arrived from **236**, *score* ◯◁.

She picked it up. It was a small screw. Where had it come from?

She looked all around for other screws of the same size, and then she saw that there were screws like this holding down the oak plank that was the top of the window seat.

She looked to see if any were missing. All the screws were tight, but − yes, in the middle of the front side there was a hole without a screw.

Her mind flashed back to last night, when she had hidden under the bed and seen someone fiddling about by the window, bending over the polished oak seat. She remembered the puzzling little noises − clinks and squeaks. It could have been the top of the seat being fastened down with screws.

She tapped the seat. It sounded hollow. It must be a kind of box, and George's mind was set on unscrewing the lid to find out what was inside.

Could this be a clue to the mystery? George ran downstairs, found a screwdriver, ran back with it to the bedroom and locked the door in case Block came snooping about.

What would she find in the window seat?

Go to **232**.

243

If you've arrived from **239**, *score* ⌒.

'Let's risk it,' Julian said. 'Come on, follow me, everyone!'

He took his torch and sat on the edge of the window seat, let himself go, and landed at the bottom of the hole, very jarred and shaken.

He looked up at the anxious faces peering down at him. 'It's a tough jump. You'll have to find a rope and fix one end up there. No – hang on. I can see some niches cut into the sides of the hole. You can climb down.'

They went down in turn, feeling for the niches with their feet, and landed safely. George went last, missed the last two footholds and landed with a sprawling bump.

Cautiously, they groped their way along the low tunnel. It led to a flat space in the middle of a flight of rough stone steps. Should they go up or down?

'I'd like to go up,' Julian said. 'It could lead to some of the tunnels and secret places under the house. Mr Barling could easily have hidden them there.'

'My instinct says go down,' Anne said.

'Why?'

'I always trust my instinct.'

If you think they should go down, go to **249**.
If you think they should go up, go to **254**.

244

'I can't see anything.' George leaned inside and ran her hand over the inside of the seat. 'Wait – what's this?' She pulled out a scrap of blue cloth that was caught in a splinter on one of the boards.

They all bent over it.

'Uncle Quentin would never wear bright blue like that,' Julian said. 'He always wears those old browns and greys . . .'

'That's because he's a brilliant scientist,' George snapped, defending her missing father, who might be in some terrible danger.

'. . . but Sooty had a blue shirt,' Julian continued. 'Was he wearing it yesterday?'

They all tried to remember. Sooty liked clothes, and wore different coloured shirts all the time.

'When he let me in at the side door, I'm sure he had on a blue shirt.' George wanted her find to be a clue. 'Yes, I'm sure.'

Go to **235**.

245

They went back up the steps to where Mary's hairband hung on the projecting stone. She reached up to take it down, but Julian said, 'Leave it as a marker. Something tells me we'll be back this way before long.'

At the bottom of the hole they pulled themselves up quite easily by the niches in the sides, and were glad to be back in the sunlight coming in through the window of Sooty's bedroom.

Julian shut down the lid of the window seat and replaced the screws.

'So if Block comes in, he won't know we've found the secret exit. I bet he unscrewed the lid to let Mr

Barling in and then screwed it down again after he'd gone, as George saw when she was under the bed.'

Go to **248**.

246

'We'll have to go back down,' said Julian reluctantly.

Anne opened her mouth to say, 'I told you so,' but thought better of it.

Until there was space to stand up and turn around, they had to crawl down backwards, Julian going behind them on his stomach, to give them some light from the torch. Now they were level with the place where the narrow side passage led off into the unknown.

Julian said, 'Let's try that way.'

George fished in her pocket for a toffee and said firmly, 'I'm sure we should go back down.'

If you think they should go back down, go to **249**.
If you think they should try the narrow passage, go to **260**.

247

Meanwhile, what was happening to Uncle Quentin and Sooty?

Mr Barling had drugged and gagged Uncle Quentin, so that he couldn't struggle or call for help.

Then he had dropped him down the hole under the window seat. He was badly bruised by his fall.

Then Mr Barling had dropped poor Sooty down after him, and climbed to the bottom of the hole himself, using the niches in the walls.

'This serves your stepfather right,' he hissed at Sooty, 'for trying to work against me.'

His servant was down there, a hard-faced man who helped him half-carry, half-drag the two captives along the tunnel and down the flight of stairs to the cave, which led to the network of secret tunnels.

Mr Barling produced a ball of string. 'Tie the end to that beam supporting the roof of the cave,' he told his servant, 'and let it unravel as we go. I know these tunnels, but Block will have to bring food to the prisoners tomorrow, and he won't know the way.'

Go to **250**.

248

After lunch, served by Sarah, who said Block was still in bed with one of his headaches, Julian went down to ask Mr Lenoir if he had contacted the police yet.

'I want to go down to the police station, and I want Block to come with me,' said Mr Lenoir. 'He doesn't answer the bell that rings in his room. I can't think where he is.'

'I'll go and find him,' Julian said willingly. He ran up the stairs and pushed open Block's door.

Block was still asleep. Julian called him, loudly, because he was supposed to be deaf. When the man didn't move, he went to the bed and put his hand on the lump of shoulder under the bedclothes.

It didn't feel like a person. It was soft and squashy. *It wasn't Block!* The 'head' was a large, tight ball of rags, black to look like Block's head half under the sheet. The 'body' under the blankets was a lumpy mass that might be a bolster, or something like a rolled-up sleeping-bag.

If you think it's a bolster, go to **255**.
If you think it's a sleeping-bag, go to **261**.

249

If you've arrived from **246**, *score* ◁◁.
If you've arrived from **260**, *score* ◁◁◁.

'We should leave a marker here, in case we get lost,' suggested Dick, as they stood on the steps and looked at the opening to the tunnel that led to the window seat. They left Mary's pink hairband hanging from a jutting-out stone so they could be sure of the way back. Going on down, the steep steps took them at last to a small cave, out of which opened two or three of the chalky tunnels that made an underground network beneath Castaway Hill.

'Listen!' Dick whispered suddenly. 'Someone's coming!'

In the wide tunnel to the left of them they could hear the hollow sound of footsteps. Julian switched off the torch and they all shrank back into the shadows under an overhanging rock.

Go to **241**.

250

After a long and painful journey through winding tunnels and up and down slopes and steps, Sooty and Uncle Quentin were dragged into a rounded cave, dug into the side of a low tunnel. Mr Barling's lantern showed a bench with a rough blanket on it, a box for a table and a jug of water. Nothing else. This was their prison.

Uncle Quentin was thrown on to the bench, still unconscious and breathing heavily. Sooty came to himself sitting on the cold stone floor. His head ached as if he had been hit with a sledgehammer. He didn't know where he was, but he knew Mr Barling, who stood over him, and he shouted at him, 'Let me go – get me out of here!'

'Not so fast,' Mr Barling said nastily. 'You stuck your nose in where you had no business. Now you'll stay here where you can't do any damage. You're at the heart of Castaway Hill. No one knows about this passage, so don't try to get out, or you'll be lost for ever!'

He laughed in an ugly way and, taking the lantern, went quickly away with his servant.

Sooty jumped up and ran after them, calling for a light. But the lantern's glow faded and the footsteps died away, leaving only the ghost of that mocking laugh.

Sooty was desperate. He wanted to run after them, but he was afraid of becoming lost in the dark tunnels.

If you think Sooty should run after them, go to **256**.
If you think he should return to the cave, go to **263**.

251

Sooty retraced his steps. They must escape! Mr Barling was evil enough to leave them here to die. Block would never come with food. What was that Mr Barling had said about a ball of string? Sooty had vaguely heard it. Something about marking the trail . . . If he could find the end of it, perhaps he could work his way back towards the house and the astonishing pit that had opened up under the window seat in his bedroom.

If you think Sooty should look for the string and follow it back, go to **259**.
If you think he should return to look after Uncle Quentin, go to **263**.

252

'What's this got to do with me?' Uncle Quentin said. 'I'm only interested in the plan to drain the marshes and to build the houses and roads that people here need.'

'Exactly.' Mr Barling was still smiling, deep shadows in the lines of his face, his eyes glittering in the lantern-light. 'And my business depends on the marshes and the mists. If a proper harbour is built here, my ships won't be able to creep in unseen.'

'You're mad!' Uncle Quentin protested. 'Those things can't go on now. You're living in the past.'

'I know.' Again the sinister laugh. 'I love the excitement and danger of it. And I hate you, and all your kind. I know that Mr Lenoir wants to buy your plans for drainage, but he won't!' Mr Barling raised his voice. 'Because you will give them to me. Tell me where they are, and Block will get them.'

'And if I won't?'

'Then I may have to force you,' Barling said nastily.

Uncle Quentin went pale. A rage of energy exploded through Sooty, and he jumped off the bench to attack Mr Barling.

'No, Sooty, wait!' Uncle Quentin tried to hold him back.

If you think Sooty should attack Mr Barling, go to **258**.
If not, go to **264**.

253

He had heard of underground lakes. He struggled and splashed, terrified that he would slip further forwards into the freezing black water.

Gradually he pulled himself back until he was once more kneeling on dry ground. He squeezed as much water as he could out of his shirt and sat back on his heels.

Should he try to find the string again and go on, or should he leave it and go back to the cave?

If you think he should go back, go to **263**.
If you think he should look for the string, go to **266**.

254

'I trust my reasoning,' Julian said loftily, and he led them up the steep stairs. Soon a narrow passage went off to the right, but he went on up, searching the steps above him with his torch, because he had no way of knowing how far under the house they were, and he didn't want to bump his head on the underside of a trapdoor.

The steps grew rougher. They had to step over fallen stones. The roof grew lower, and they had to bend until they were crawling on hands and knees.

'Blow!' muttered Julian. 'Rock fall.'

His torch showed him that the way ahead was blocked by fallen stones and rubble.

Go to **246**.

255

If you've arrived from **261**, *score* ⌣.

Julian tugged the blankets off the bed and found a large bolster, cleverly moulded to look like Block's heavy body.

'So *that's* the trick Block plays when he wants to slip off secretly and pretend he's still here,' said Julian. 'It *was* Block in the tunnel, and it *was* Block who George saw through the window yesterday, talking to Mr Barling. *And* he's not deaf! He's a sly, clever rogue – and probably a criminal!'

Go to **247**.

256

Sooty felt he couldn't just sit in the cave and wait for something to happen. How dare Mr Barling think he could get away with all this! Shouting with fury, he ran and stumbled along the dark passage, feeling the walls on either side. His desperate voice echoed hollowly back to him.

Then he stopped. Silence. Only the sinister *drip, drip* of water from the roof somewhere, and the sound of his own harsh breathing. Loneliness overwhelmed him. He was alone in the treacherous maze under the hill.

Then he remembered George's father, unconscious, perhaps badly hurt, and with no one but Sooty to save him.

Go to **251**.

When they both woke up, Sooty's luminous watch face told him that they had slept all night and it was morning, but it was still dark. It would always be dark in this prison.

Uncle Quentin seemed wide awake now, and quite sensible, so Sooty told him what had happened. He was amazed and furious.

'I shall take it to court,' he said, 'if we ever get out of here.'

'We can't, without a guide,' explained Sooty. 'These tunnels can be really treacherous.'

After some time they heard footsteps. Lantern-light came down the passage and into the cave, and behind it were Mr Barling and Block.

Sooty raged at Block, and Block's face went red in the flickering light, and he snarled, 'You hold your tongue!'

'Ah! So you *can* hear! That proves it. My step-father believes you're deaf, but all of us began to suspect it was a fake. What a lot of secrets you must have heard, from people who thought you couldn't hear.'

Mr Barling was talking to George's father. He sounded very cunning. 'Don't agitate yourself,' he told the angry Uncle Quentin. 'I have a proposition to make. First, I know why you came here, and about your interest in Mr Lenoir's experiments.'

'Spying!' Uncle Quentin accused him.

'Yes, and Block too,' Sooty put in. 'Eavesdropping. Opening letters.'

'I expect you know I'm a smuggler,' Mr Barling went on. 'All sorts of goods can be smuggled in here, because of the secret paths through the dangerous marshes. When it's safe to come ashore I send signals to the ships from the tower at Smuggler's Top.'

'Or Block does,' Sooty said bitterly.

'Exactly. Clever boy, Pierre.'

Go to **252**.

258

If you've arrived from **264**, *score* ◯◁.

Nothing could stop Sooty. He hurled himself at Mr Barling and began to pummel him with his fists. Cursing, Block dragged the boy off and pinned his arms painfully behind his back. Sooty kicked out wildly and screamed at the top of his voice.

From nowhere, a powerful furry dynamo crashed through the entrance to the cave and leapt at Block, snarling and growling.

Timmy!

The two frightened men could do nothing against the angry dog. Soon they were running down the tunnel as fast as they could. Timmy chased them, barking triumphantly, and then came back to the cave, bounding joyously at Sooty and licking his hands and face. Uncle Quentin was surprised to see Timmy, who had not been invited to Smuggler's Top, but he had to admit he was thankful that George had disobeyed him.

'Poor old fellow,' Sooty said to Timmy. 'You look half-starved. Wherever you were, I hope you caught a few rats and mice to eat, and found some water somewhere. Here – good thing Block brought us some food. It's all yours.'

Go to **262**.

259

Sooty passed the entrance to the cave prison and went on, feeling up and down the walls on either side with his hands, and bending down to feel along the floor. He was almost ready to give up when he found it, a loose end of thick string hanging from the end of a timber in the wall.

He followed it up and over the timber, and carefully along the left-hand wall, at knee height. It was awkward having to walk crouched over to keep his hand on the string.

The floor of the tunnel sloped suddenly sideways, and he fell, and lost the string. He knelt up, groping for it, shuffled forwards, and fell again, on to his face into an ice-cold pool of water.

Go to **253**.

260

Eventually, Julian started off with the torch down the side passage. Rather than split into two groups, the others had to follow. In the moving light and shadows from the torch they lost a sense of direction, but the mysterious passage, with its damp walls and a slippery floor, led them on.

In a little while they came to some steps.

'Good heavens.' George stepped forwards and pounced on something lying on one of the steps. 'There's the toffee I fished out of my pocket and dropped. We've walked in a circle.'

She put the toffee in her mouth, and they went on down.

Go to **249**.

261

The blankets were tucked down tightly around the fake body. Julian was starting to undo them when he heard a tread on the stairs, and Sarah's voice called, 'Mr Block?'

Julian came quickly out of the room.

'Mr Lenoir sent me up here to wake him up, but he's sleeping heavily.'

'Ah, poor fellow. He do suffer with his head.' Sarah went into her own room, and Julian heard her opening and shutting drawers, so he had to go downstairs until she went away. He filled in the time by looking in the landing cupboard where he knew that Sooty kept the tartan sleeping-bag he brought to school for camping weekends.

The sleeping bag was there, rolled up in a corner.

When Sarah finally came down, Julian nipped upstairs again.

Go to **255**.

262

The dog ate ravenously, wagging his tail. When he
had wolfed down the last crumbs of bread, he went
to the mouth of the cave and whined.

'You want to go, don't you?' said Sooty. 'So do
we, and I'll bet you can lead us back. Come on, boy,
take us back to George!'

'Will he get us lost?' George's father was still
weak and shaken.

'He knows these tunnels through and through,
and he knows the way to the marsh. He may take us
down there, or to the house, but either way we'll be
free!'

If you think Timmy heads for the house, go to **273**.
If you think he heads for the marsh, go to **267**.

263

If you've arrived from **251**, *score* ◠ ◠.
If you've arrived from **253**, *score* ◠ ◠ ◠ ◠.
If you've arrived from **266**, *score* ◠ ◠ ◠ ◠ ◠.

With a sigh, Sooty decided that the only thing was
to go back to the cave. He could get hopelessly lost
on his own, and at least Uncle Quentin would be
another human being for company – when he woke
up.

Back at the cave, Sooty could hear Uncle Quentin's harsh breathing, and sometimes a low moan. He stumbled over to the bed in the dark and shook him.

'Wake up!' he said urgently. 'Talk to me! I'll go mad if I can't talk to someone – wake up, oh, please, wake up!'

The man stirred at last. He moaned, tried to sit up, and fell back on to the hard bench. 'What's happened?' he asked feebly. 'Who's there?'

'It's me, Sooty. You came here to visit my father – Mr Lenoir, remember?'

'Where is he? Where's the light?' Uncle Quentin's hand groped feebly about, looking for a bedside lamp, and knocked Sooty on his still aching head. 'Oh dear,' he moaned. 'Oh, I'm so tired, so . . .' He was asleep again, poor man, already deeply asleep. Sooty was exhausted too, and cold and aching. Nothing for it but to creep under the blanket with George's father and try to sleep for a while.

Go to **257**.

264

With a giant effort, Sooty was able to control himself. He wanted to hurl himself furiously at Mr Barling, but the man was so much bigger and stronger than him. What use would he be to George's father if Mr Barling knocked him out again and left him senseless?

He must bide his time and think about what to do, look for any chance to trick the men and escape. He sat down by the bench, hunched over.

'Such a hero,' Block sneered at him. 'All bluster and no bravery. When I was your age, I could stand up and fight like a man, but look at you!'

Sooty hung his head to hide his burning face. His fingers clenched into fists.

'You see, you're at my mercy,' Mr Barling told Uncle Quentin. 'I'm top dog now, and if you don't give me the papers, I'll . . .'

His threatening voice was cut off as Sooty jumped up and went for him.

Go to **258**.

The others had been telling Mr Lenoir about the hole under the window seat, and seeing Mr Barling and Block together.

Mr Lenoir was staggered. 'I trusted Block, but Mr Barling must have put him into this house as a spy, because my plans to drain the marsh would spoil his smuggling business. This is a terrible crisis.'

'If only we could find Timmy!' George said.

'Who's Timmy?'

So they told him about the dog, and, to their amazement, Mr Lenoir said, 'It's true, I don't like dogs, because I was bitten by one when I was a child, but if I'd only known, I would have boarded him in the town for you.' Mr Lenoir kept being much less cross and scratchy and much more understanding.

While he went to telephone the police again, George and Julian and Dick and Anne decided to go through the secret door in his study and whistle and shout for the dog in the passages beyond.

Go to **270**.

He stood up and felt his way up the wall. Perhaps the string went higher, to avoid the water. Perhaps it went off down a side passage. Feeling nothing, he stood on tiptoe, reached higher up the wall, and slipped into the water again.

When he got himself out he was soaking wet and discouraged. So much for trying to escape . . .

Go to **263**.

267

With Sooty's hand on the dog's collar, and Uncle Quentin holding on to the back of Sooty's shirt, they set off into the darkness. Poor Uncle Quentin's feet were bare, and as a chill mist began to creep into the tunnel he shivered in his thin pyjamas.

It was a joy to walk out into open space and fresh air, but the mist was so thick over the marsh that they could hardly see anything.

'Leave it to Timmy,' Sooty said. 'He can take us safely around the hill to the road, can't you, boy?'

For answer, Timmy stopped dead, then threw up his head with his ears pricked. He whined uneasily, then barked, and ran back into the tunnel.

'Timmy! Timmy! Come back!' The mist deadened Sooty's voice. 'Timmy!' But he was gone.

'We can't go over the marsh by ourselves,' Sooty told Uncle Quentin. 'It's too treacherous. Timmy's probably gone after a rat. We'll have to wait here until he comes back.'

Wearily, they sat down on a rock. 'I wonder what

the others are doing,' Sooty sighed. It seemed a lifetime since they had all been together.

Go to **265**.

268

Quickly, George slid behind a large copper urn that held a potted plant. She heard Sarah put down a tray and open the sideboard drawers to get out knives and forks. Sarah moved slowly, and it took her ages to lay the table. George was getting cramped. She peeped out. Heavens! Sarah was making a great business of folding the napkins into special shapes.

At last she was finished, and went out. George slid back under the sideboard and squeezed painfully through into the dark space between the two flaps.

She had been gone for ages. What if the others hadn't waited for her?

If you think the others have waited, go to **280**.
If not, go to **274**.

269

If you've arrived from **279**, *score* ⌒.

The opening she chose led her down a wider passage, high enough for her to stand up straight.

George started down it, calling, but suddenly there was a squeaking noise, a rush of wings, and something brushed against her hair. She pressed herself against the wall in terror, her heart beating fast.

'Get hold of yourself, George. It's only a bat,' she told herself sternly. But a bat was bad enough to make her not want to go on. She turned away from where the bat had flown and began to grope her way back. Which way now? She could either go straight on or turn right.

If you think she should go straight on, go to **279**.
If you think she should turn right, go to **286**.

270

The panel slid back. They went through, past the wide opening to a downhill path and into a narrow passage that led them, around corners and up steps, to the blank wall behind the cupboard in Sooty's bedroom. They went slowly back down.

'Remember Sooty telling us that there was a secret door from this passage to the dining-room?' George said. 'I think it should be about level with here.'

She felt along the bottom of the wall, and suddenly her hand went through as a small flap door opened with a groaning squeak.

'Look – Timmy might have pushed through here.'

'He'd get stuck.'

'No, he wouldn't. I could go through.' George was on hands and knees, pushing the flap with her head.

'Come back!' Julian said. 'You don't know where it leads. Stay with us.'

If you think George should go through the flap door, go to **277**.
If not, go to **282**.

271

It was a length of thick string running along the wall at one side of the tunnel.

'Do you think Block and Mr Barling followed the string to take them to the place where Sooty and my father are prisoners?' asked George excitedly. 'Come on! Let's follow the string!'

Cautiously and quietly, because they didn't know where the enemy might be lurking, they followed the string around sharp corners and mysterious side tunnels. At one point Anne stepped off the path and was up to her knees in icy water. She screamed, and Julian put his hand over her mouth as George and Dick pulled her out.

Eventually, the string led them to a rounded cave. 'Look!' Julian shone his torch all around the walls. 'This must have been the prison.' There was a rough bench with a tumbled blanket, an overturned lantern and a smashed jug on the floor.

'There must have been a struggle,' George said. 'Good old Sooty! Do you think he hit Mr Barling?'

Go to **276**.

272

If you've arrived from **283**, *score* ◯↰.

Tied up in a corner, the tight knots cutting into her wrists and ankles, George shouted with all the strength of her voice: 'Timmy! Timmy! Help me! Timmy!'

Go to **281**.

273

They followed Timmy along many different tunnels, up steps and around narrow, rocky corners, where Uncle Quentin had to hold on to Sooty's arm to keep his footing.

'Will we soon come out?' he asked uncertainly. 'The dog seems to be taking us uphill.'

'Don't worry,' Sooty reassured him. 'He'll find a way out. Trust him.'

But Timmy, following the memory of the first days when he was here, had taken them up and up to the secret door that led into the cupboard in Sooty's bedroom. He didn't understand that there was no way in there now. At the top of the last steps he waited, wagging his tail, for Sooty to push open the door.

Sooty tried, but the slab of stone wouldn't budge.

'We used to come and go this way,' he told Uncle Quentin, 'but the handle's gone from the other side and it's locked. Come on, Timmy, down to the marsh!'

Go to **267**.

274

If you've arrived from **287**, *score* ⌀.

As she crawled back through the second flap, George said, 'No luck, I'm afraid,' but no one heard her. The others had gone off without her, and taken the torch. How mean! George wasn't sure which way to go. In the dark, she was confused. She felt her way along the wall again, until her groping hands discovered that the passage had come to an end. There was an opening on her right and one on her left. Which way had the others gone? Should she go on, or go back to try to find them?

If you think she should go left, go to **269**.
If you think she should go right, go to **279**.
If she should go back, go to **286**.

Eventually they chose the steps, and Dick went first, picking his way down the steep, uneven stone slabs.

Then he felt for the next step with his foot – and it wasn't there. He sat down and his legs swung in open space.

Julian's torch showed a sheer drop, like a precipice, where the steps had broken away.

'A metre and a half, not more,' Julian guessed. 'You and I and George and Timmy can drop down. Anne can jump, and we'll catch her.'

At the bottom, a sandy path swung around to the right, on the level. They walked in a wide semicircle before the path began to rise and grow stonier. After a steep climb they came out into a wider space.

'Another one of those meeting points of tunnels.' Dick was still leading.

'Idiot, it's the *same* meeting point,' Julian said. 'We've climbed up the slope that I wanted to go down. Dick's path and mine are just a big loop.'

Go to **285**.

'If he did,' Julian said grimly, 'Mr Barling's coming back for more.'

They all heard his voice, then heard footsteps in the tunnel where the string was.

Julian switched off the torch and they all huddled

at the back of the cave. A brilliant light exposed them.

A curse, and then Mr Barling roared, 'Who's there? Oh, it's you, you young fiends. I might have known.'

'You might have known we'd come to rescue George's father and Sooty.' Julian stepped forwards and faced the man boldly, although he could hardly see him behind the powerful torch. Block stood menacingly in the shadows behind. 'Where are they?'

'Search me,' Mr Barling said. 'When that vicious brute of a dog attacked us, we ran.'

'Dog?' cried George in wonder. 'My Timmy? Wouldn't you know he'd come to the rescue?'

'The game's up, Mr Barling,' Julian said. 'Mr Lenoir knows everything, and at this moment he's talking to the police.'

'In that case,' Mr Barling snarled, 'you can all stay down here. Got that rope, Block?'

Block stepped forwards and grabbed George roughly.

'Let me go!' she screamed, struggling. 'I'll call Timmy – he always comes to me, and he'll protect me!'

'If you call that dog,' Mr Barling said with cold calmness, 'I'll shoot him.' He patted a bulge in his jacket pocket. 'I'm armed, you see.'

It was the most dreadful decision of George's life. If Timmy couldn't rescue her, she might stay, bound and gagged, down here until she died. If she called him, Timmy might die.

If you think she should call Timmy, go to **272**.
If you think she shouldn't, go to **283**.

277

George kicked her ankles free and squeezed through the flap, grazing her shoulders. She crawled on through a low, dark space that must be the thickness of the wall, and bumped her head against another flap at the end.

Cautiously, she pushed it, crawled through and fell on to the dining-room floor. She was under the sideboard. She could see the legs of the dining-table and the chairs. If Timmy had come through here, he would certainly have run through the house and found her. She had better go back.

At that moment she heard steps on the wooden floor outside the dining-room, and Sarah's voice calling, 'I'll just get the table laid, Mrs Lenoir.'

Should George let Sarah see her?

If you think George should hide from Sarah, go to **268**.
If not, go to **284**.

278

They chose the slope, and Julian led them down it, expecting it to get steeper and steeper until it came out at sea level by the marsh. The tunnel swung around in a wide arc to the left, and soon it levelled out and became a smoother, sandy path.

'This is easy.' Julian walked faster. 'Come on, you lot, hurry up.'

They speeded up, and ran into the back of Julian when he stopped dead without warning.

Go to **289**.

279

If you've arrived from **269**, *score* ◯↲ .

The way she picked turned out to be little more than a shallow alcove. Almost at once, George came up against a wooden panel. Another secret door! She pushed it and prodded it, but it wouldn't budge. Then she tried to make it slide sideways.

Very slowly, the door began to move. Cautiously, George put out a hand into the darkness beyond.

At once she touched something rough and unyielding. It was a solid wall. Someone must have bricked up the tunnel to prevent anyone using the secret door.

George closed the panel and turned back. Which way should she go now? Left or straight ahead?

If you think she should turn left, go to **286**.
If you think she should go straight on, go to **269**.

280

If you've arrived from **287**, *score* ◯↲ .

As George crawled back through the second flap, Anne said, 'You've been ages. Any luck?'

George shook her head. 'None. Timmy must have gone some other way. But *where*?'

Go to **282**.

281

Out at the edge of the marsh with Uncle Quentin and Sooty, Timmy was too far away to hear George's voice. But he stopped and flung up his head and listened. He could hear nothing, but he *knew*. This wonderful dog's instinct, and his great love for his friend George, told him that she was in danger.

Go to **288**.

282

If you've arrived from **280**, *score* ⊂⊐ ⊂⊐ ⊂⊐ .
If you've arrived from **286**, *score* ⊂⊐ ⊂⊐ ⊂⊐ ⊂⊐ .

'Look!' Dick said suddenly. 'Here's another door. Just the same, only bigger.' He pushed at a wooden panel set flat into the wall of the passage. It flapped open, and beyond they could see a tunnel that ran steeply downhill.

'This looks promising,' said Julian, peering through the opening. 'Come on, George.'

They all went through into the tunnel, which broadened out into a space they recognised.

'Of course!' George said excitedly. 'This is the pit where we used to let Timmy down in the laundry basket so we could take him for a walk.'

It made them feel closer to Timmy. In all this bewildering maze of passages under the house, it was encouraging to find a familiar place.

Soon they recognised something else.

'There's the bottom of the steps we came down after we left the hole under the window seat,' Dick said. 'Look – isn't that the tunnel we saw Mr Barling and Block go into?'

Julian shone his torch into the mouth of the tunnel. 'Gosh!' he exclaimed. 'What on earth is this?'

Go to **271**.

283

George couldn't call Timmy, couldn't call him into this horrible trap, so she stayed furiously silent while Block tied her up securely with rope.

Now Block advanced on Julian, but as he reached for him Julian jumped to the side and lurched against Mr Barling. He fell against the bulging jacket pocket. It was a soft bulge – a scarf or a cap. As the smuggler grabbed at him, Julian swung away and yelled, 'He hasn't got a gun! Call Timmy, George!'

Go to **272**.

284

Sarah was comfortable and friendly. Not treacherous, like Block. As she came into the dining-room, George crawled out from under the sideboard and stood up.

'Ooh, how you frightened me!' Plates and glasses on Sarah's tray wobbled and jingled.

'Sorry. I was looking for a red pen I lost,' George invented wildly. 'I lent it to Dick, and he could have dropped it anywhere.'

'I saw a nice red pen in the pantry,' Sarah said. 'I'll show you. Just help me lay this table first, will you?'

Go to **287**.

285

If you've arrived from **275**, *score* ᗧ.
If you've arrived from **290**, *score* ᗧ ᗧ.

They decided to try George's way. She went ahead with Timmy, and the others followed, squeezing between the ledges of rock.

'Skinny Mr Barling might follow us here,' Anne

said, 'but Block would get stuck, and serve him right.'

The path got damper. Water dripped on them, and at one place they had to forge an underground river, mysterious and phosphorescent, under the black rocks.

At last a glimmer of daylight came, mist swirled into the tunnel, and they groped through it eagerly to come out at the bottom of the hill by the marsh. Freedom at last!

Go to **291**.

286

If you've arrived from **269** *or* **279**, *score* ⌒.

She had taken only a few steps when she heard her name being called: 'George! George! Where are you?'

It was Julian. A moment later she saw torchlight, and there were all the others coming to meet her.

'Sorry,' Julian explained. 'We didn't mean to desert you, but Dick thought he heard Timmy barking, so we went to investigate.'

'Any luck?' George asked hopefully.

''Fraid not. How about you?'

George shook her head. 'None. Timmy must have gone some other way. But *where?*'

Go to **282**.

Blow! What a waste of time, when George wanted to get back to the others. She tried to hurry the job, but Sarah was very slow and thorough, straightening the silver that George laid, and polishing George's finger marks off the glasses.

Then George had to go down to the pantry and wait while Sarah looked for the pen and couldn't find it, then wanted George to climb on a chair to get something out of the top cupboard.

At last, she sped away up to the dining-room, and through the flap under the sideboard.

She had been gone for ages. What if the others hadn't waited for her.

If you think the others have waited, go to **280**.
If not, go to **274**.

Block had tied up Julian and Dick, and Mr Barling was advancing on the terrified Anne, cowering on the bench, when out of nowhere a thunderbolt of energy and rage shot into the cave, snarling like a wild beast, and sank his teeth into Mr Barling's shoulder. Screaming, the two frantic men ran out of the cave, without their torch, and stumbled away, cursing, into the darkness.

Go to **290**.

'Well, I'm blowed.' Julian shone his torch upwards on a sheer wall of rock. 'I can see the top, but none of us could climb up there – especially the girls.'

'What do you mean?' George started to jump and claw at the rock face, vainly trying to get a hold; but they had to go back the way they had come.

Go to **285**.

290

Anne untied Dick, who untied Julian, who untied George. Timmy jumped all over her, whining with joy. And George, who never cried, found that tears were pouring down her face.

'Come on, Timmy!' Julian said. 'Get us out of here. Take us to Sooty!'

Wagging his tail, the dog led them forwards to an open space with many openings off it. Which way? Timmy sniffed about, uncertain.

'This way, Tim,' Julian said. 'It slopes downhill towards the marsh.'

'I don't like the look of it,' Dick said. 'Try those steps over there.'

'No, here.' George urged Timmy towards a narrow opening between two rocks, where water dripped.

If you think they should go Dick's way, go to **275**.
If you think they should go George's way, go to **285**.
If you think they should go Julian's way, go to **278**.

291

A shout made them look up. To their joy they saw Sooty and Uncle Quentin waving from the entrance to a cave a little higher up.

Soon they were together, and exchanging breathless news. Timmy led them around the hill to the road and they trudged up to Smuggler's Top, exhausted and filthy from their adventures.

Sarah nearly had a fit when she opened the door.

She called out, and Mrs Lenoir and Mary came running to embrace Sooty.

'You're a brave man.' Mr Lenoir shook hands with Uncle Quentin. 'I'll take you straight to the police inspector to give evidence against these two criminals.'

'When I've soaked my poor feet.' Uncle Quentin laughed. 'I've been going through all this without shoes!'

That evening, the inspector and his men went into the maze of tunnels to search for Mr Barling and Block. No sign of them, so the inspector asked George if she would send her dog down there again to round them up for arrest.

Timmy soon found Mr Barling and Block. He chased them up to the house, to be led away in handcuffs, then the Famous Five sat down to a late supper.

Uncle Quentin was taking them home tomorrow. It was goodbye to Smuggler's Top – the end of an amazing adventure.

'Not the end of adventures though,' Julian said with his mouth full of pie. 'There's always another one around the next corner!'

Will the Famous Five have more adventures together?

Yes, of course they will! And perhaps YOU will be there again, too.

How many red herrings have you collected?

0–25	Very good indeed! The Famous Five must have been glad to have you with them.
26–50	Promising. Perhaps your next adventure with The Famous Five will be even more successful.
51–75	You took a long time getting there, didn't you? You'll have to do better than that to keep up with The Famous Five!
More than 75	Oh dear! Perhaps you should go back to the beginning of the story and try again.

Join the Famous Five on more of their exciting adventures in *The Famous Five and You*.